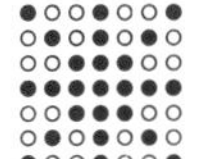 Tony Cragg

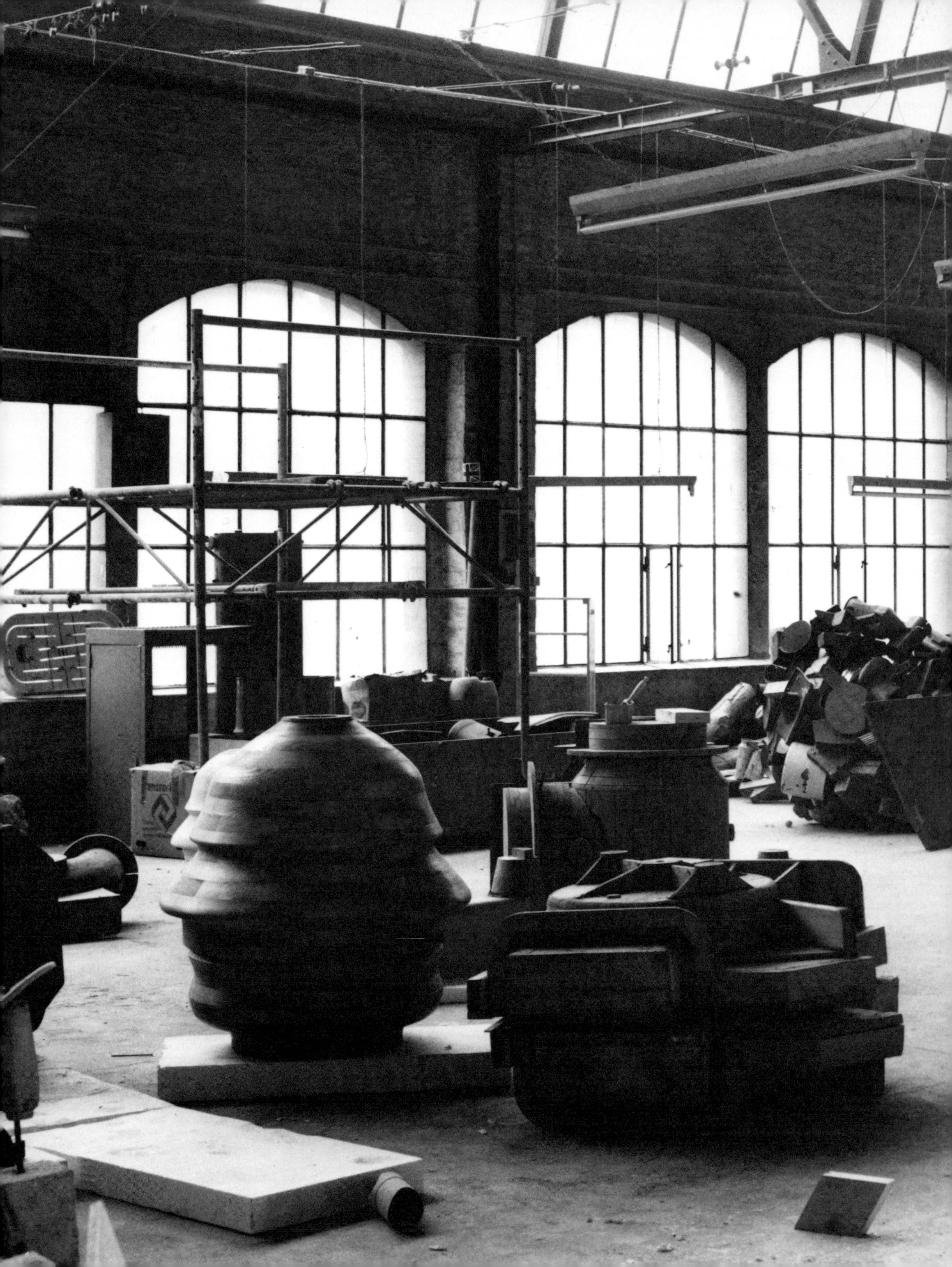

TONY CRAGG

XLIII
BIENNALE DI VENEZIA

26 June – 25 September 1988

THE BRITISH COUNCIL

Published by The Visual Arts Department
THE BRITISH COUNCIL
11 Portland Place London W1N 4EJ

ISBN 08-6355-0681

Distribution for Europe,
excluding Great Britain and Italy:
Buchhandlung Walter König, Köln.

Commissioner for the British Pavilion:
Henry Meyric Hughes

Deputy Commissioners:
Malcolm Hardy
(Deputy Representative/Arts Officer
The British Council, Italy)
Ann Elliott
(Exhibition Officer,
The British Council, London)

Exhibition Assistant: Gillian Adam

Photography:
Graziano Arici, Thomas Backhaus, Ann Elliot,
Dorothea Fischer, Max Grünert,
Nanda Lanfranco Salvatore Licitra,
Enzo Ricci, Friedrich Rosenstiel,
Jörg Sasse

Designed by
Klaus-W. Richter and Tony Cragg

Printed by
Druckerei Heinrich Winterscheidt GmbH,
Düsseldorf

. . . . . . "Trying to pierce the darkness of political idealism with some wild, despairing urge toward truth? Sitting day after day supine in a rigid chair and infinitely removed from life staring at the tip of a steeple through the trees, trying to separate, definitely and for all time, the knowable from the unknowable? Trying to take a piece of actuality and give it glamour from your own soul to make for that inexpressible quality it possessed in life and lost in transit to paper or canvas? Struggling in a laboratory through weary years for one iota of relative truth in a mass of wheels or a test-tube " . . . . . .

F. Scott Fitzgerald 1922
The Beautiful and Damned

Preface

Once again, we have decided to present a monographic exhibition in the British Pavilion. After showing two of our most distinguished painters in successive Biennales, we have chosen one of our leading sculptors to represent Britain at the XLIIIrd Biennale. Tony Cragg may by familiar to visitors to other international events, such as Documenta and has already had important museum and gallery exhibitions in Europe and America, but almost all the work in this exhibition is being shown for the first time. A few earlier pieces and the catalogue itself serve to underline the essential continuity in the artist's approach to his subjects, but we intend that the display should evoke a fresh and immediate response from the viewer. Cragg conjures up a myriad of images in a multitude of materials, which delight, intrigue and test our reactions.

I am indebted to the members of our Fine Arts Advisory Committee and its Chairman, Sir Alan Bowness, for advice over the selection of the artist and stex-scope of the work to be presented. The generosity of those who have lent pieces from their own collections, is warmly appreciated, and I thank them for helping us to assemble this exciting selection of Tony Cragg's sculpture. Their names are listed on page 41. I should also like to thank the following for their part in the realisation of the exhibition: Thomas Backhaus and Joe Holmes, Tony Cragg's studio assistants; Nicholas and Caroline Logsdail and the staff of the Lisson Gallery, London; David Ricks, the British Council's Representative for Italy, in Rome; and Anthony Smallwood, Annamaria Campari and Elena Daniotti from the British Council in Milan.

We are most grateful to the Henry Moore Foundation for their generous contribution towards the cost of the catalogue. This is particularly apposite, since Henry Moore's sculpture first won international acclaim at the British Pavilion in the 1948 Venice Biennale. I should also like to thank the Greek writer, Demosthenes Davvetas, for his informative and poetic background essay, and Catherine Lampert, the new Director of the Whitechapel Art Gallery, for the insight with which she has described individual works in the exhibition, and set them in the wider context of Cragg's œuvre. We have enjoyed particularly close and efficient collaboration with Mr Klaus-W. Richter and the printing house, Heinrich Winterscheidt GmbH, Düsseldorf, in their work on the catalogue and related graphics.

I am especially grateful to the two British Deputy Commissioners: Malcolm Hardy, Deputy Representative and Arts Officer, Italy, for all his efforts in refurbishing the pavilion and coordinating arrangements at the Italian end; and Ann Elliott, the Exhibition Officer in this Department who has supervised the entire project in every detail and at every stage, with consummate skill.

Our warmest thanks go to the artist himself, for offering us the collaboration, understanding and creative impulse without which nothing could have been achieved. The work will speak for itself and for Tony's irrepressible joy in doing naturally what he does so well.

Henry Meyric Hughes
Director Visual Arts Department

A Dictionary of Dematerialisation

MATERIALS 1

In the work of Tony Cragg materials have the function of a kernel, but kernel in the Greek sense of the word *pyrene*, which derives from the word *pyr*, meaning fire. This etymology suggests that materials are chosen by the artist not only for their visual or compositional power, but also as signs of energy which give birth to the world, as signs of a fire which knows how to burn and how to create. Materials are the energy, the fire, the motion; they are a visual reality which is not limited by the 'optical', but also appeals to the invisible. They are the traces of that which exists but is invisible.

MATERIALS 2

Each kind of material is its own world, its own microcosm; each breaks into particles, each particle into atoms, each atom into whatever results from further splitting. Materials, in this case, are the evidence of an artist's experience as he wanders through the world; they are his weapon and his defence against the world, his language and his tool, his goal and his object of desire. Tony Cragg's materials are his passion for knowledge, for technology, but also, at the same time, proof of his critical stance towards knowledge and technology. Materials are the obsession which hunts him down wherever he goes. They are his Erinys and his Moira. They are ultimately whatever he has chosen as his field of action, the place where he develops his energies. They are the objects which undergo his inspection and handling.

MATERIALS 3

Materials are the creation of Charm. Charm has decided to elect Tony Cragg as her interpreter. To facilitate matters she uses materials as part of her strategy: they become the bait, the scent-trap, the mermaid's song which lures the artist and implicates him in the process. Charm uses materials to create visions for the artist, to take over his spirit and all other dematerialised parts of his being.

Often Charm is hiding in the very composition of materials: she takes the shape of one material's elasticity or polymorphism and in this way demands that Tony Cragg be organically bound up with material. It should therefore not come as a surprise when we are faced with the following scenario: just as the material moves, so the artist moves, each of them a part of the other, of the same body, of the artist's body.

CHEAP MATERIALS

One other characteristic of Charm is that she loves to inhabit cheap materials; she loves nature's refuse, the scattered litter of the streets, of storage areas, the garbage, or whatever remains from factories and other such stuff. The artist is forced to wander amidst the discarded materials searching for Charm's scent or song, for her traces. And when he is certain he has found them, he becomes aggressive, wild; he battles with the material-trace, he does not want to lose it, he does not want it to get away. The result of this match is first and foremost the empowerment of the artistic subject with regard to the discarded material. And then the metamorphosis of the material: Tony Cragg alters it to such an extent that it actually becomes one and the same as Charm.

This metamorphosis of cheap material into something valuable is a constructive act: it shows the potential of the subject which has been chosen by Charm to be her interpreter.

THE OBJECT

In the case of Tony Cragg the object functions like a magnet: it pulls the artist, attracts his attention and his energy. The subject in this relation is characterised by surprise and curiosity: he is amazed by the possibilities which hide inside the object, but he also has the curiosity to test how far his own subjective potential goes in this repeated use of the object.

This process carries inside it the seed of an Overthrow: the artist wants to overthrow the heretofore fixed order's use of the object, and to offer a new use. However, in order to succeed in overthrowing the object, he must be well acquainted with it, he must get inside it and learn its structures. And this is exactly what Tony Cragg does; he opens himself up, breaking down personal supports and learning from the same object new ways of using artistic space.

Artist + Object = a marriage of information, emotion and energy. Here is one equation which in the case of this English artist can easily be proven. We only need compare it with the following equation: Artist + Object = archaeological research of one on another, and vice versa.

That is to say, in both the above equations, the artist uses the object as a field of discovery of new energies, but also at the same time as an "eye" which enables him to penetrate deep inside himself, to find his deepest secrets.

NATURAL MATERIALS – ARTIFICIAL MATERIALS

As the meaning of "nature" changes to comply with the shifting sands of cultural history, the "artificial" element becomes a stronger and stronger reality. This double reality of "nature" and the "artificial" envelops Tony Cragg's work: next to materials such as stone, bronze etc., he places others such as plastic.

This kind of behaviour aims at broadening artistic language with non-artistic materials. It expands the alphabet of possible materials, of possible techniques for using the materials, and in so doing constructs an artistic stance.

In the case of Tony Cragg this stance has its own trademark: while up until now many artists have been identified with one particular material, and their names have even become synonymous with the use or consistency of that material, Tony Cragg has never allowed himself to get trapped in that situation; he has been careful to express himself through a myriad of materials. This tendency has to do with the logic of the "opening" which governs his work. In each of his works the material makes an impact, not by virtue of its density, mass or weight, but, on the contrary, because of its flexibility, pliancy and lightness.

The objects-materials, one next to the other, unfold in the artistic space and take it over, creating a work which is airborn, which broadcasts the artist's truth with ease. This work does not eulogise the material; it is not there to praise the material, but rather to praise the dematerialisation of material, to sing its decodification.

Beyond the realm of the object or the material, Tony Cragg concerns himself mostly with spirituality. He illustrates how the spirit can use the material to its own advantage, and how the artist, the subject of this dematerialisation, uses the object-material as a spiritual support, and nothing more.

IMAGE – SCULPTURE

Each material by itself can be an image. But two materials combined, one next to the other, comprise another image, or rather, not *an* other image but *all* other possible images.

Tony Cragg's sculpture is made up of many images, or one image constantly decentreing itself, one image in the process of breaking into many. It is structure in abundance and a structure of abundance; it is all the forms a familiar structure can take.

Cragg's structure-image is an elastic, open, polymorphic organism. It is the "contents" as they explode; it is the "contents" in their multiplicity of contents; it is the centre of its own fragmentation. This sculpture is not only the product of the artistic subject's experiences and observations, it is the product of a synthesis of spirit, body, memory, observations and vision. It is whatever has witnessed the experience of the artistic subject in the world.

DECONSTRUCTING – RECONSTRUCTING

Tony Cragg deconstructs the already known images of the collective memory; he deconstructs and reconstructs the structure of these images; he reveals them in their transparency, in their fragmentary unions, as if he were trying to put flesh and bones on shadows.

Tony Cragg deconstructs an already existing artistic thought; he thinks deconstructively; he thinks the deconstruction in order to succeed in reconstructing the thought, in thinking another reconstruction. In this journey without an end he uses the following human materials: logic and irrationality, realism and intuition, knowledge and emotion, the material as auditor and the material as seducer.

THE SPECTATOR

This process of deconstruction and reconstruction is a provocation on the part of the artist, but a provocation that carries within it something positive: an invitation to the spectator. He, the spectator, is asked in turn to continue the work. With his own imagination, with his own obsessions, his own visions, he constructs his own interpretation, which is the next chapter in the work's life.

This leads me to view the "gaps" that fall between the materials in Tony Cragg's works as invitations to the spectator to participate in the completion of those works.

From this fact alone it is obvious that Tony Cragg does not want to teach the spectator something; he does not want to ask questions with ready-made answers. On the contrary, he wants to provoke him with contradiction. And for this reason instead of offering him a mirror where, in seeing himself, he would "die" in self-satisfaction, he offers him signs which provoke contradictions. These are not contradictions which are exhausted in the "look", but which pass from the "look" to something deeper: they are in touch with the spectator's thought, his memory, his imagination, his emotions, his spiritual being. They are contradictions which have a metaphysical as well as a physical dimension.

VISUALISATION

Just as a telescope can make the galaxies or the moon visible, or a microscope can make cellular structures visible, or an electron microscope can make molecular structures visible or even as

Mathematics enables us to visualise cosmic energies through numbers, so Tony Cragg aims at visualisation.

He is not interested in representing a real, everyday object as it is; he is not interested in it as an object. What interests him is to visualise the disintegration of its objectification. He takes the object as a body which he happens to find in front of himself, not because it is in itself a totality, but because it is an example of that totality, a trace of that totality, of that totality's presence.

How is it possible for Tiresius the prophet to see even though he was blind. How is it possible for poets to see light in the dark? This is a question which consumes Tony Cragg. From inside his work an answer is formulated: you must see the object behind the object. You must not simply *imagine* but also *visualise*. You must reveal the body beyond the body. This English artist suggests the coexistence of the classical Greek infinitives *noein* and *oran*, meaning to know with one's mind and to see with one's eyes. In a discussion I once had with the artist, I asked him "Why do you make sculptures, or these kinds of sculptures?" He replied, "I make sculptures because they are not there."

DEMATERIALISATION

This coexistence of *noein* and *oran* is an attack upon existing art forms not only in the name of Beauty. The sculpture of Tony Cragg takes on political as well as aesthetic dimensions. It attacks centres of artistic power, intellectual power, and any way of thinking which tends towards a systematisation of material.

It is attack which is more than a formal demonstration, more than simply a general idea or architectural construct, more than an attitude (even if it is constant enough to seem like an attitude). Tony Cragg is interested in making his work *specific*, not gestural. The term *specific* has no relation to irony or ambiguity, style or formalism. It is rather a term which expresses the way Tony Cragg perceives the role of the artist. He views the artist as a *specific* person who gives *specific* answers to *specific* problems.

Tony Cragg is a *plastician* in relation both to his materials and his visions: he wants to impress himself on his materials, to shape them so that they visualise his visions. A *plastician* is someone who loves the world in which he lives, who loves to select with patience and perseverence the elements of his exploration, and then places them alongside other elements in another dimension so that the existing world takes on a new form. He broaches the "problem of nature", the problem of the natural world, of the world constructed by man, and of the world of information. Tony Cragg seems to be saying — if you want to change the world, then change the image of the world.

Demosthenes Davvetas
(Translation Karen van Dyck)

TONY CRAGG

A SELECTION OF HIS SCULPTURE 1969–1987

The first work that
Tony Cragg made at
Wimbledon School
of Art in 1969, at the
start of his studies
there. A mass of
string, cut into short
lengths, and knotted,
was distributed over
existing locations;
bathroom, sitting
room, work desk.

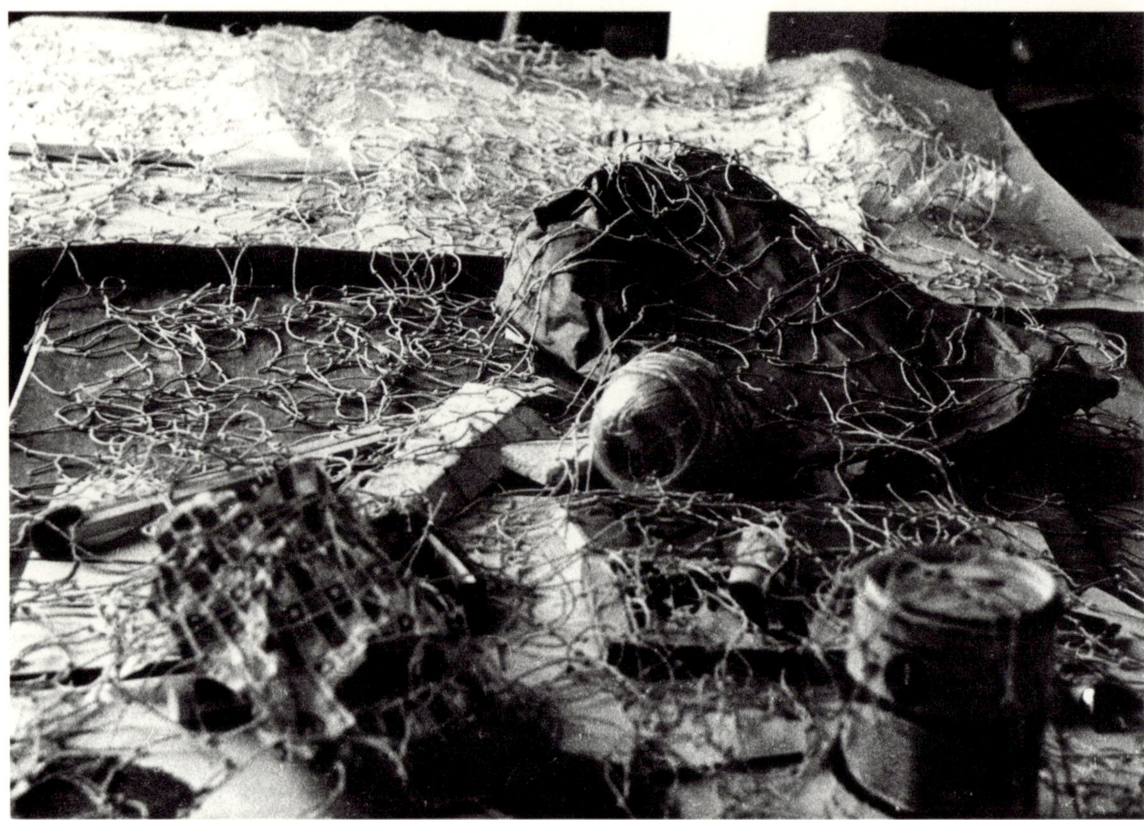

A work made in
1970 on several large
concrete cubes, the
remains of War-Time
Beach Defences, on
the beach at Climp-
ing in Sussex. These
served as a surface
for the arrangement
of beach materials,
both natural and
man-made.

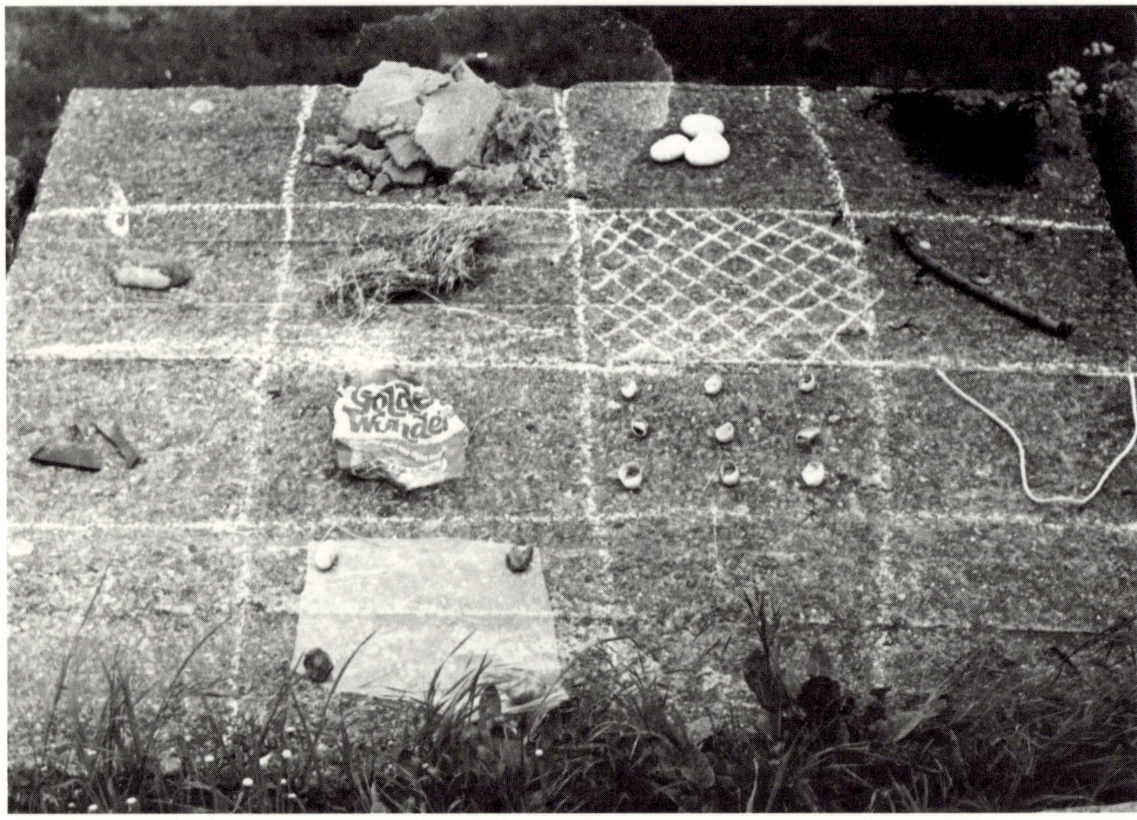

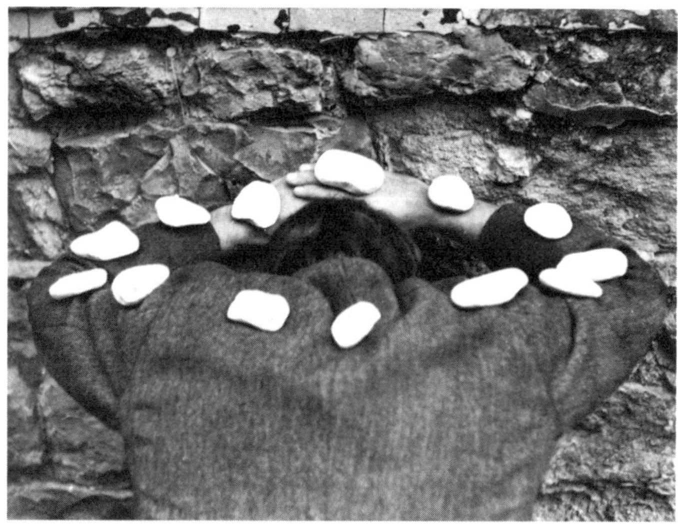

One of a number of works made whilst Cragg was working in an hotel at Bonchurch on The Isle of Wight in 1972. This was the first of a group in which the artist's own body was an essential supporting element.

A shadow in sand and a figure casting its shadow on a beach in 1972.

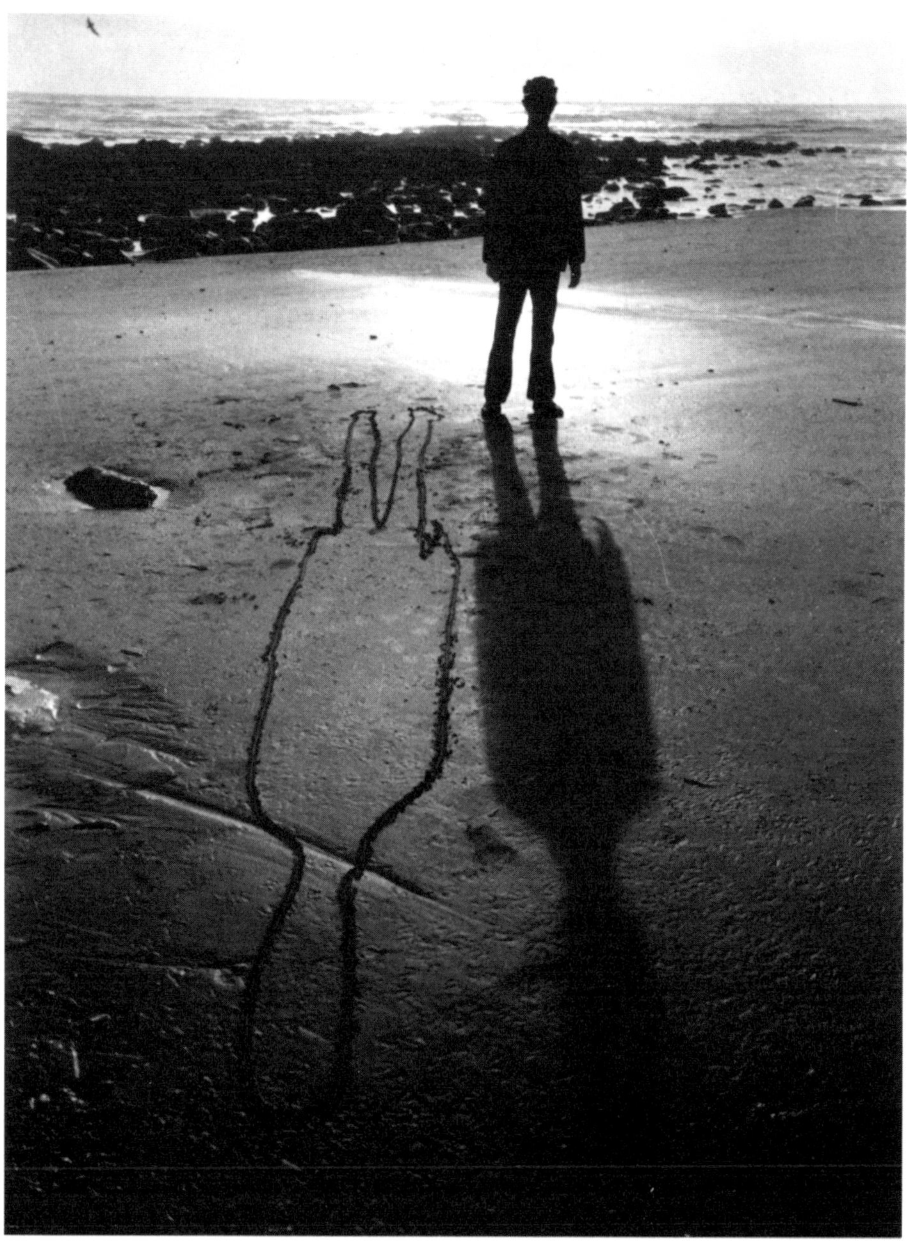

The first time that Tony Cragg worked in a studio properly equipped to make sculpture, together with other sculptors, was in 1973 at the Royal College of Art. This was the first work that he made in one of the College studios.

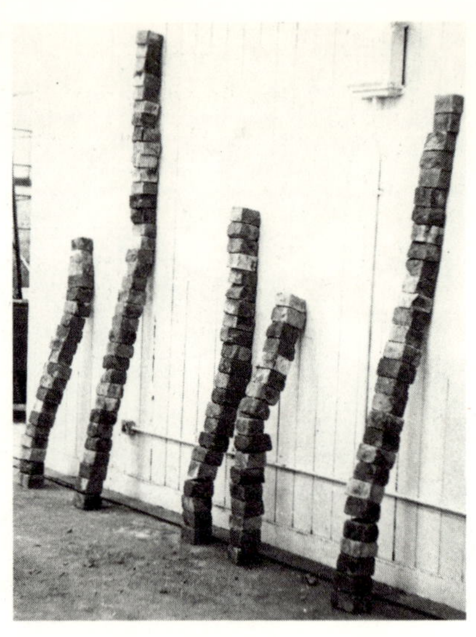

Loose wooden blocks were placed over the artist's body, or furniture. Wimbledon 1972.

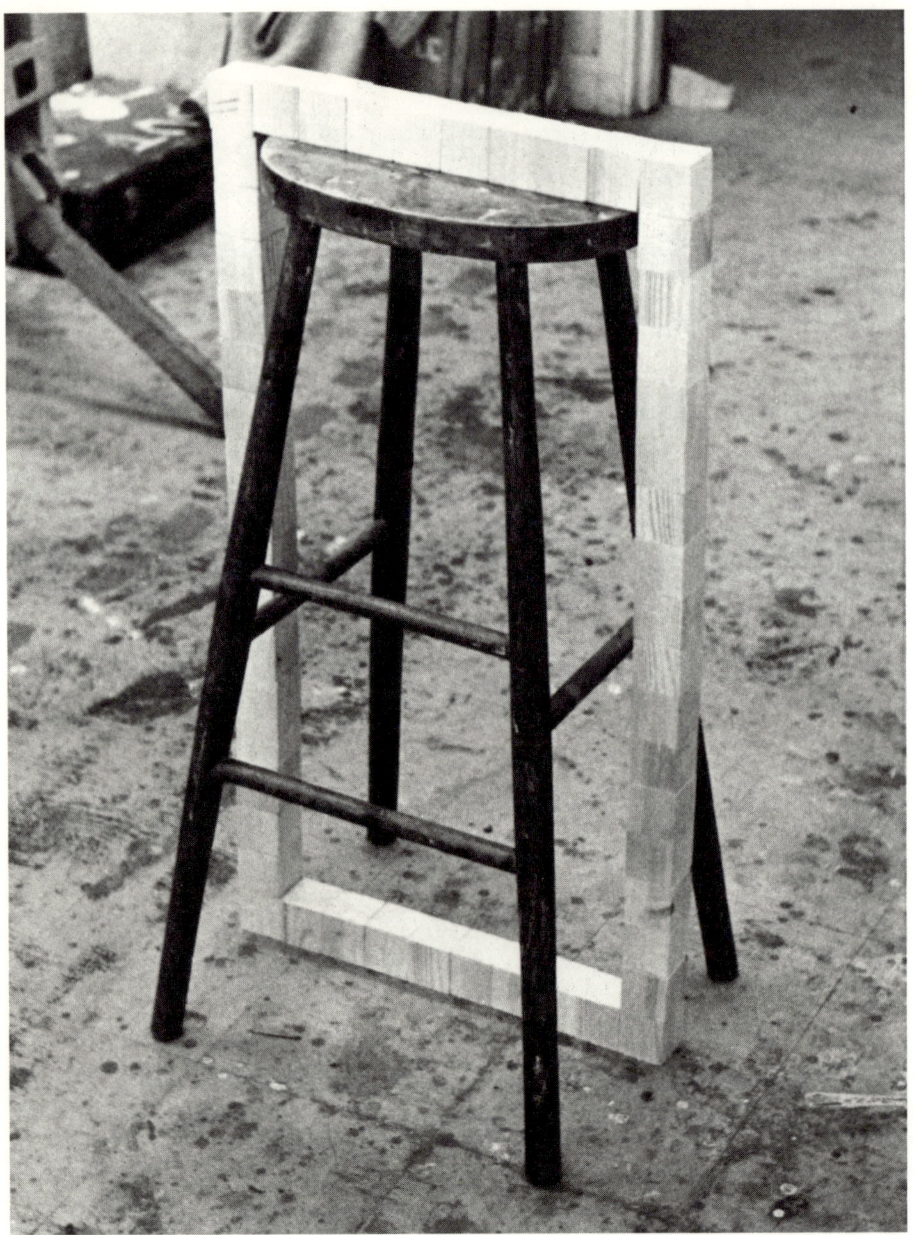

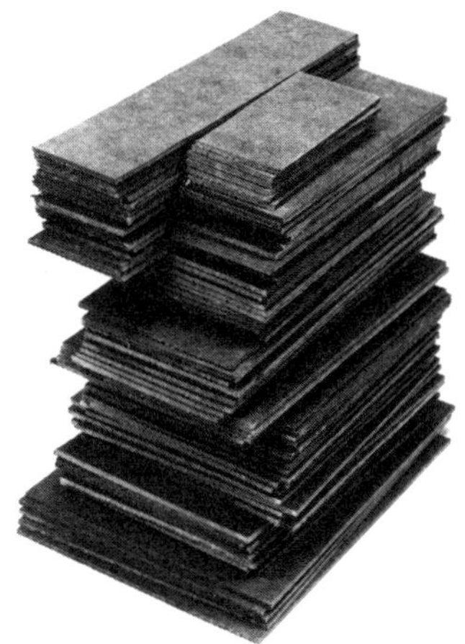

At the time of the paper bag drawing Tony Cragg had already made some out-door works, and was concerned with the relationship of objects, both natural and man-made, with the landscape, and was collecting fossils (he had, at one time, a temporary ambition to become a geologist). He made a number of small objects referring to geological structures and landscapes. This stacked structure of 1974, was made from hardboard and is about 35 cms high.

Much of Tony Cragg's material for sculpture was collected on his daily bicycle ride from his flat in the Fulham Road to South Kensington, the location of the Royal College studios. Here a very large paper bag, one metre by two metres served as a support for a charcoal drawing. This was made in 1974.

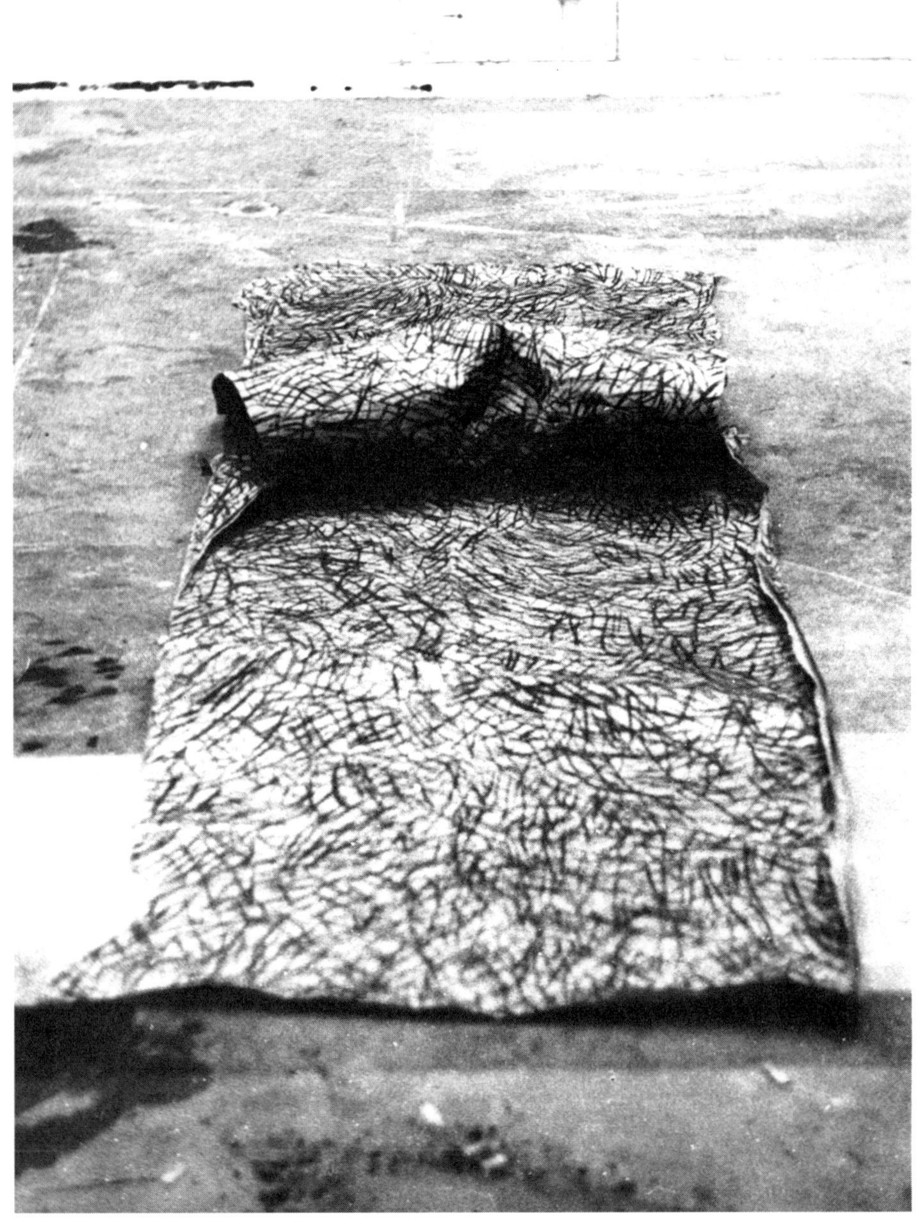

This rendering of *Four Plates* was made in 1977. The original version consisted of one plate in the studio, one plate broken, and the pieces placed in a circle of 3 metres diameter.

Fragments of the third plate were placed in the car park at the Royal College of Art and the fourth was distributed by Cragg, on his bicycle, throughout South Kensington.

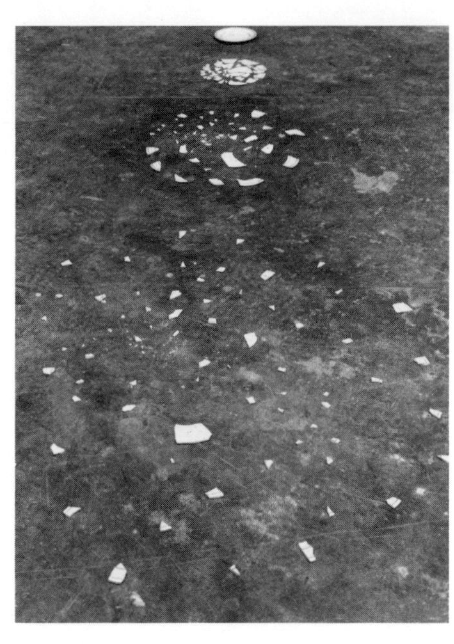

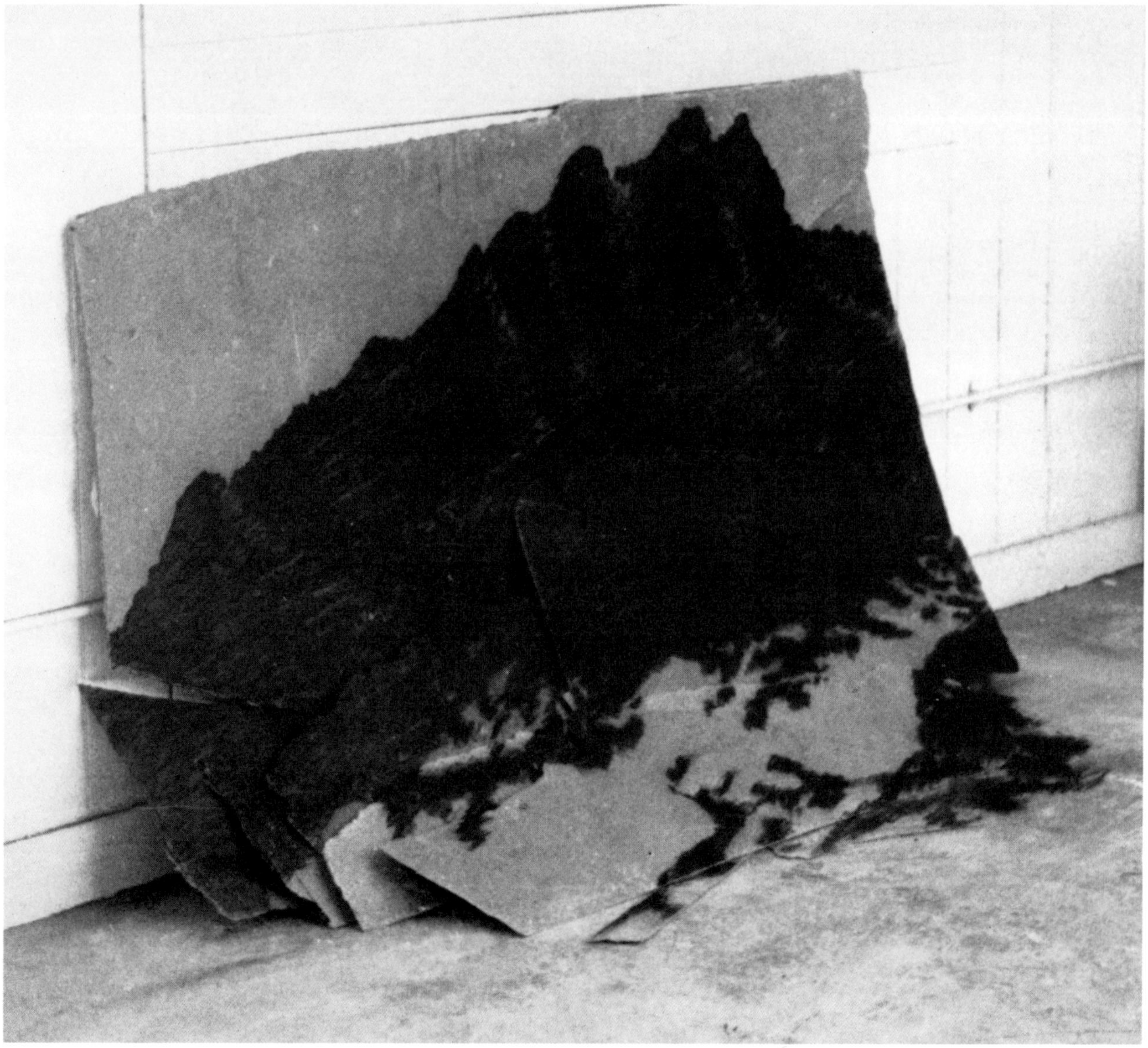

A charcoal drawing *Trefan 1975* was made on hardboard which Cragg found after a week's walking with friends in North Wales.

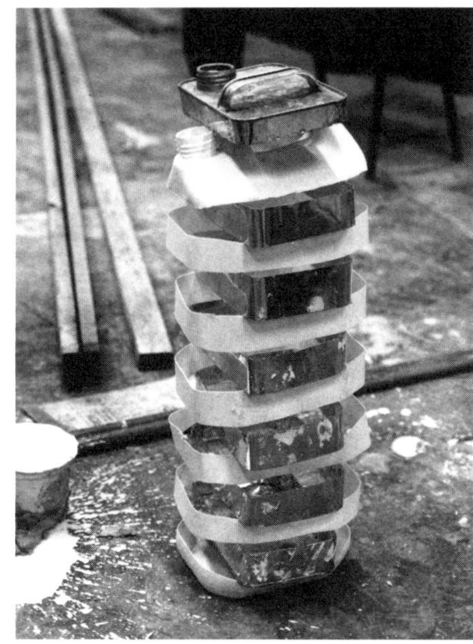

His continued on several objects that were fragmented and separated to reveal their inner volumes. A portion of these works resulted in the amalgamation of two objects, as in *Hybrid 1975*, a plastic container and a metal can. This was the first container that Cragg used in his sculpture, and the first plastic.

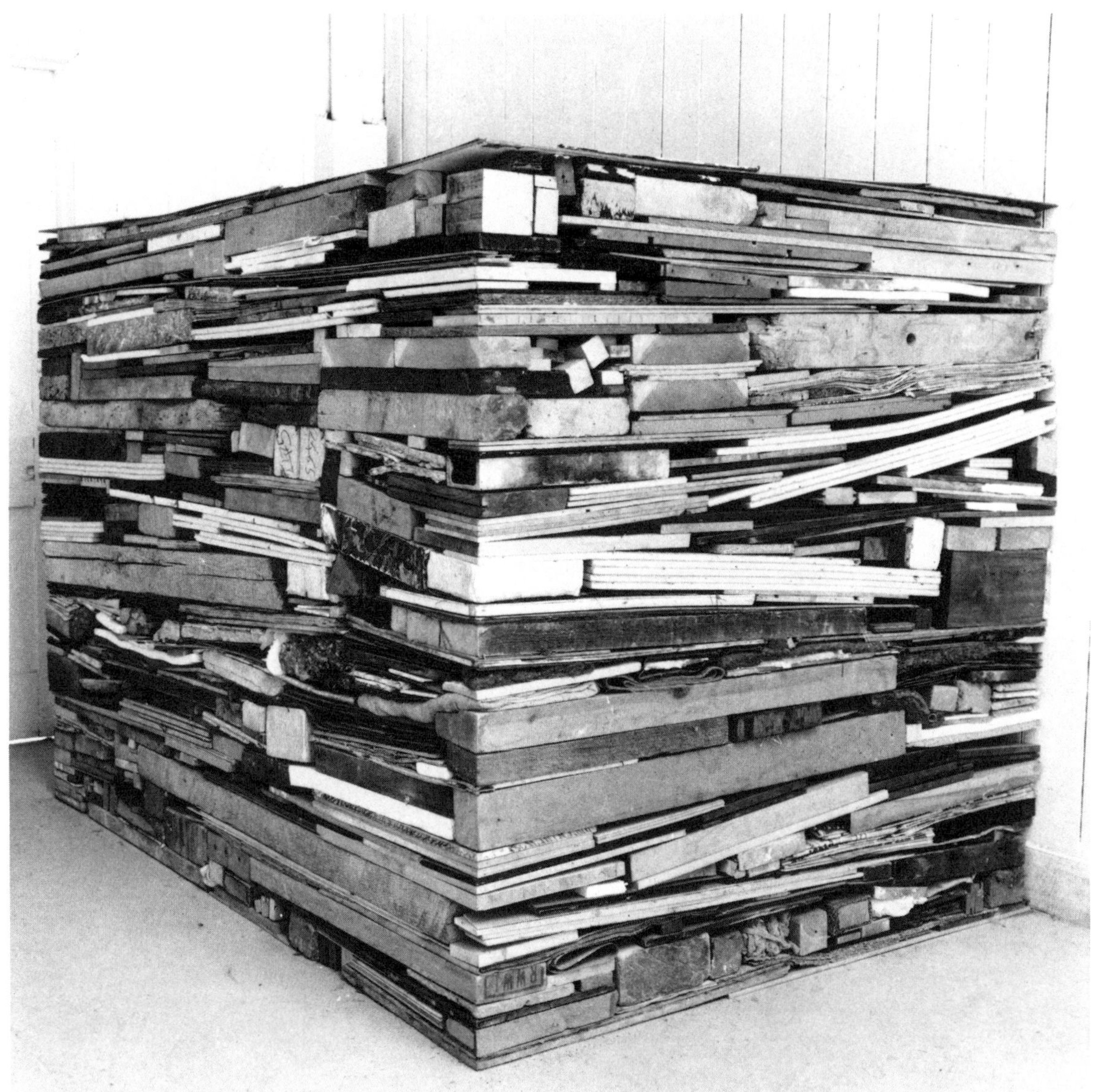

The stacks made by Cragg in 1975 before a one year stay in Metz in France were his first larger scale sculptures. The stack illustrated here was exhibited at the Royal College of Art in 1977.

Tony Cragg moved to West Germany in 1977. *New Stones Newton's Tones 1978* (collection: The Arts Council of Great Britain), was the first work made in Wuppertal, it was exhibited in his first one-man show at the Lisson Gallery in 1978.

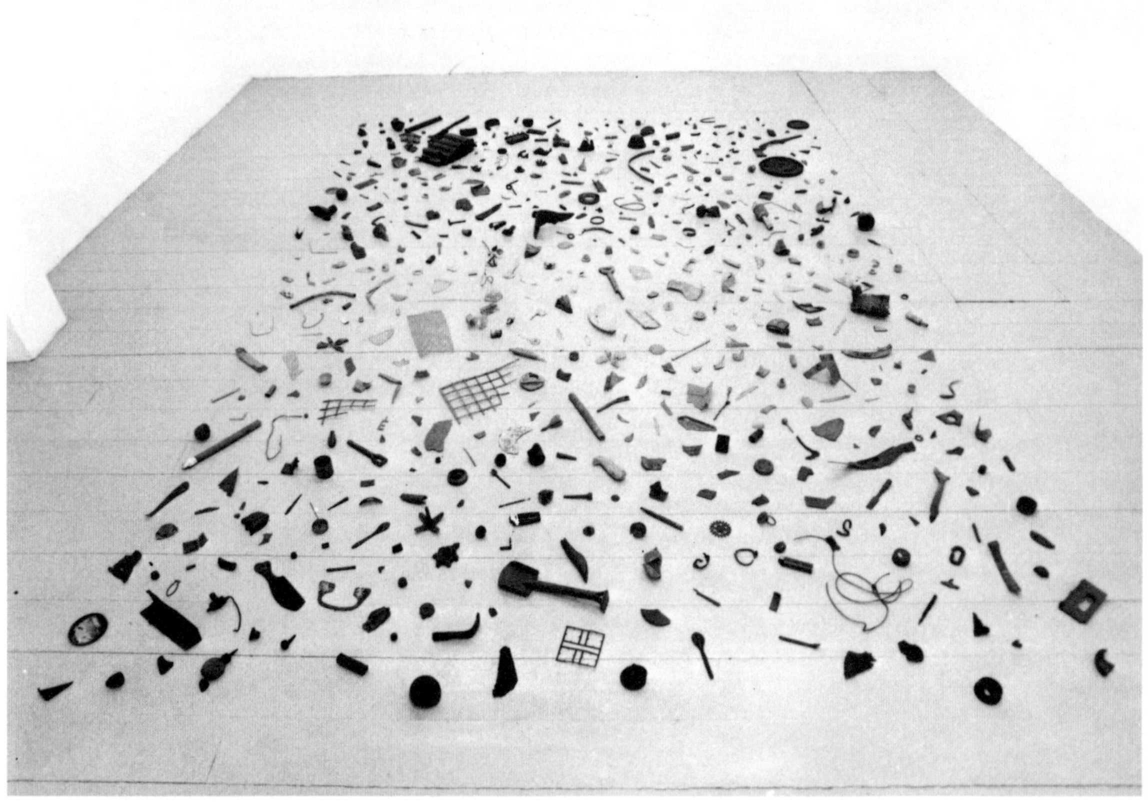

Also exhibited at the Royal College of Art exhibition was the third version of *Crushed Rubble 1977* (first version, 1976, London) (second version 1977, New York)

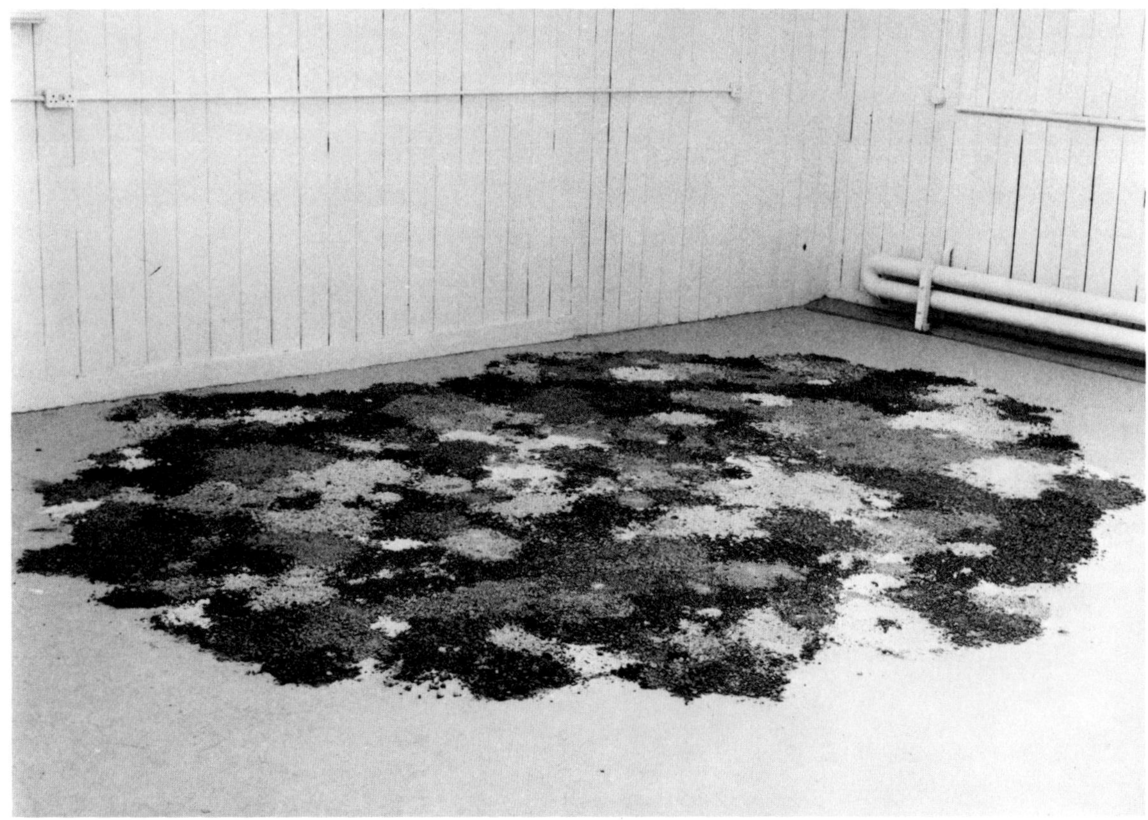

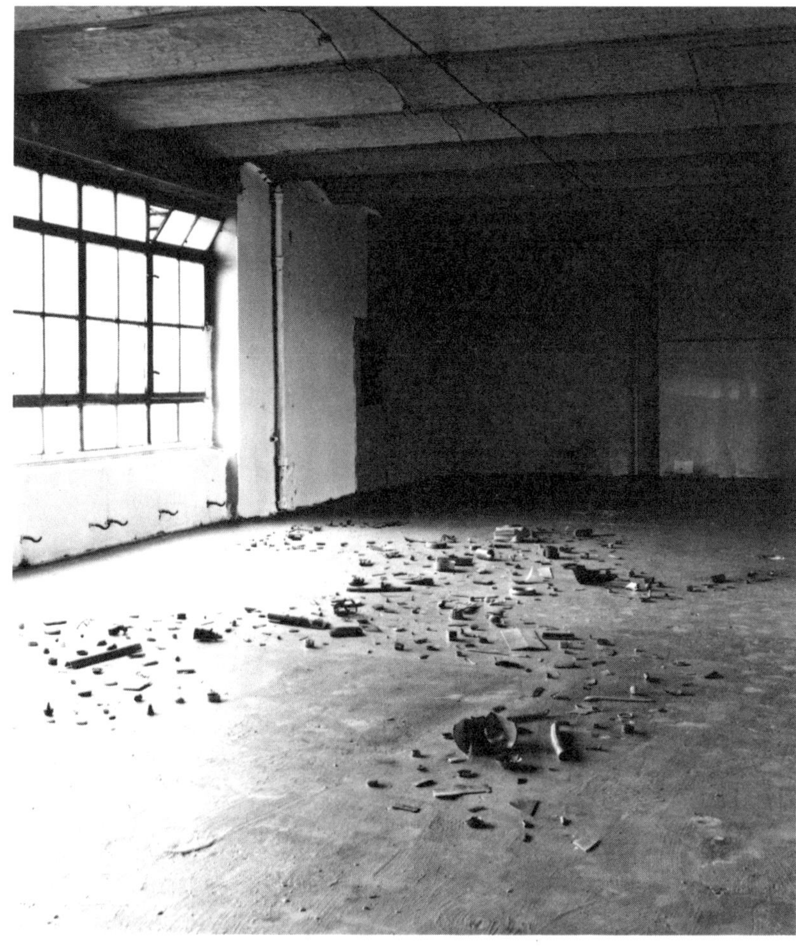

In 1979/80 Cragg was included in many group shows in Europe. *Red Skin 1979* (collection: Stedelijk Van Abbemuseum, Eindhoven), marks the introduction of a figurative element into his work, facilitated by a small plastic Red Indian toy.

The formal separation of a space, using the image of an autobahn, *Autobahn 1979* (collection: Lia Lumma) was installed at the Künstlerhaus in Hamburg.

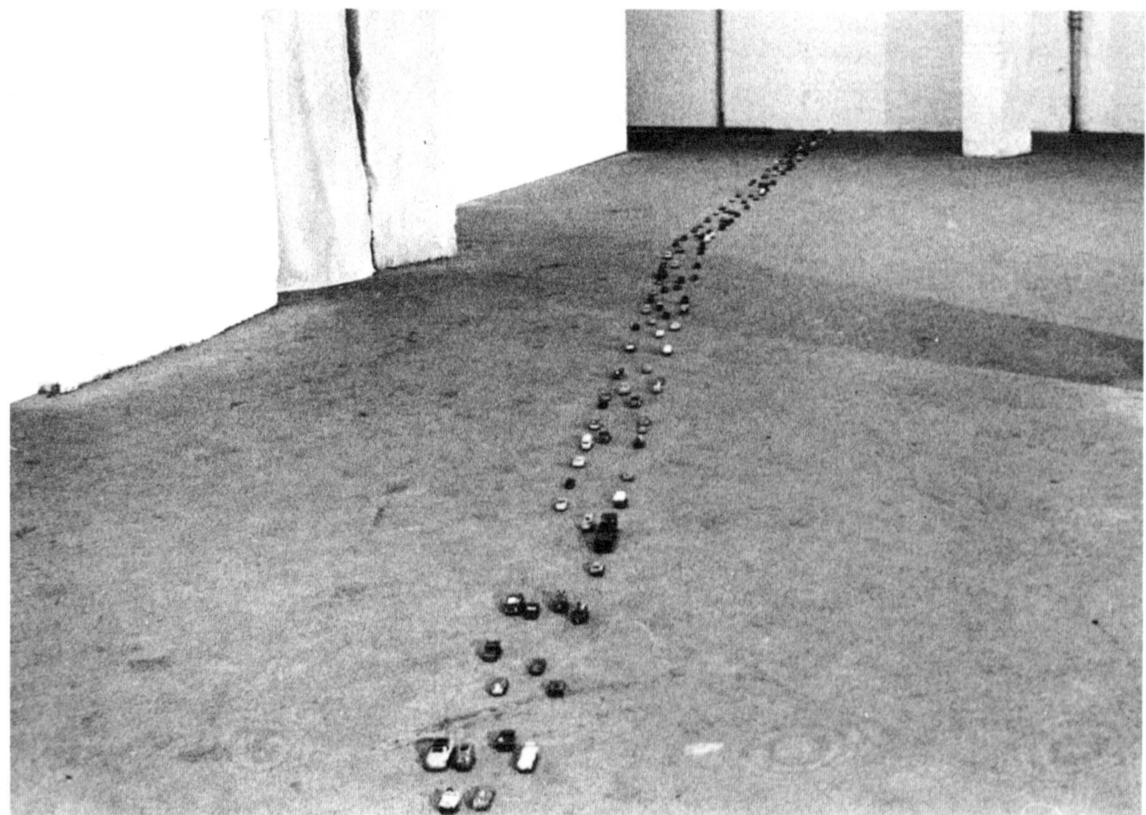

Black and White Stack 1980 (collection: FRAC, Bourgogne).

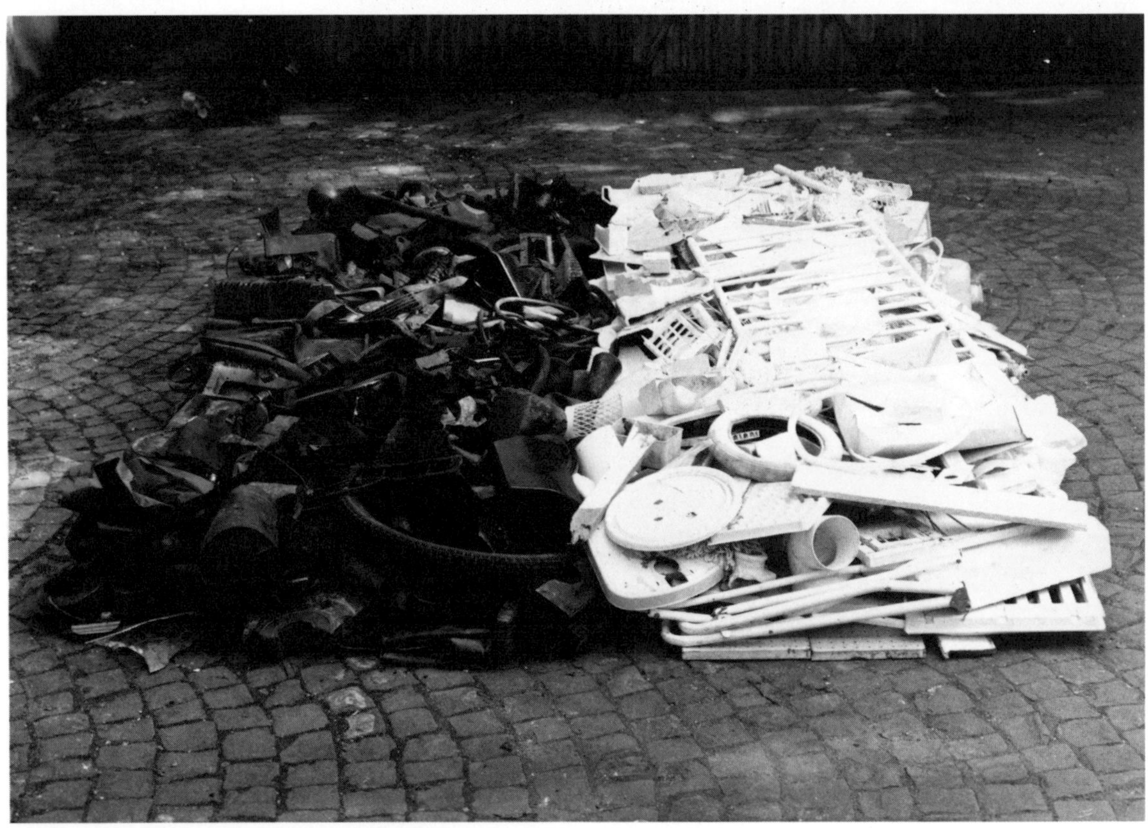

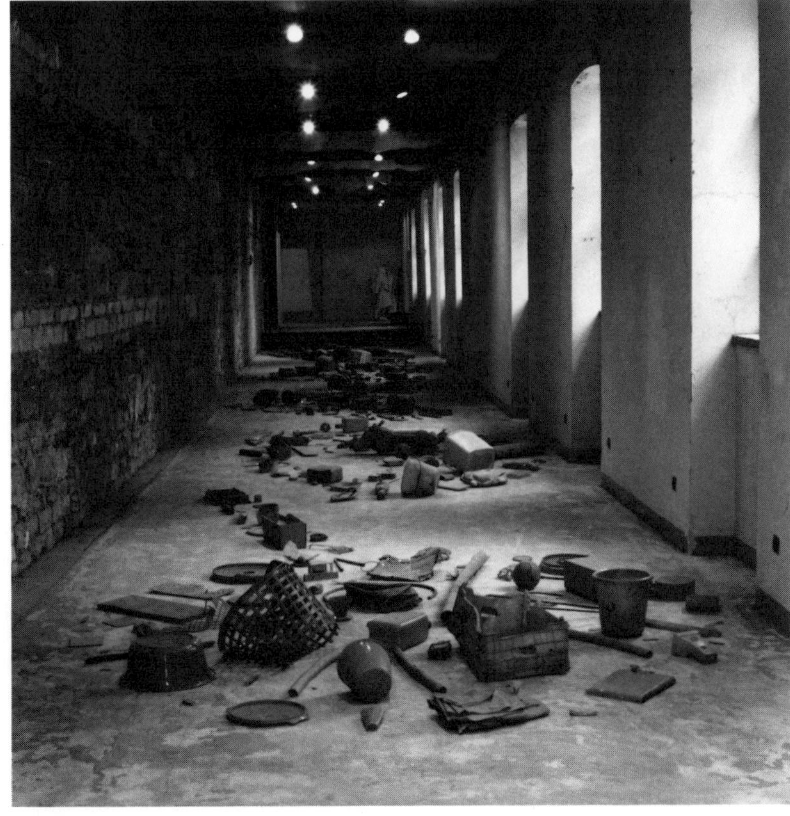

This sculpture was installed in a corridor in the Abbey of Ghent. *Five Forms on the Floor 1980*, as in the *Black and White Stack 1980*, is a mixture of tough discarded materials. Here, the sculpture is composed into five different coloured images dictated by the five objects attached to the walls; a metal saucepan, a plastic fish, a piece of paper, a green plastic bottle and a red sock.

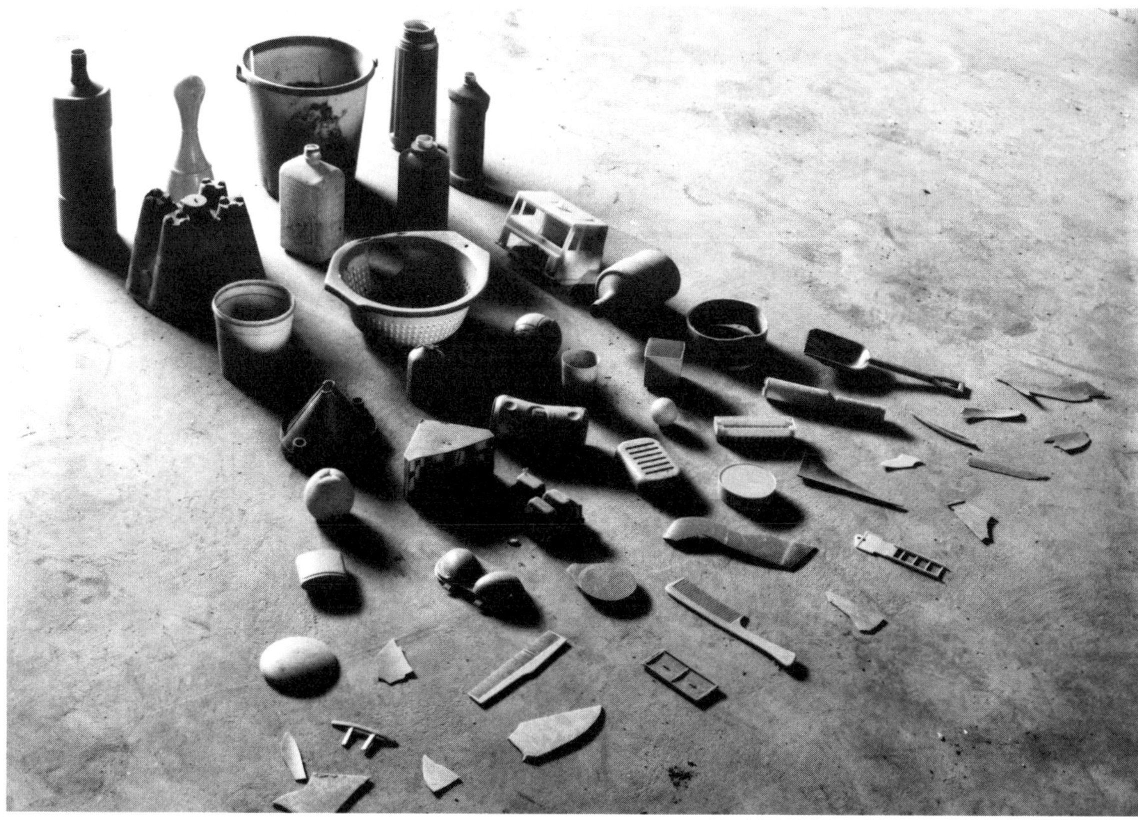

Exhibited in the Front Room Gallery in London, Cragg says that *Axe Head 1981* was a somewhat shabby work, but significant in that it introduced contour into his previously flat arrangements.

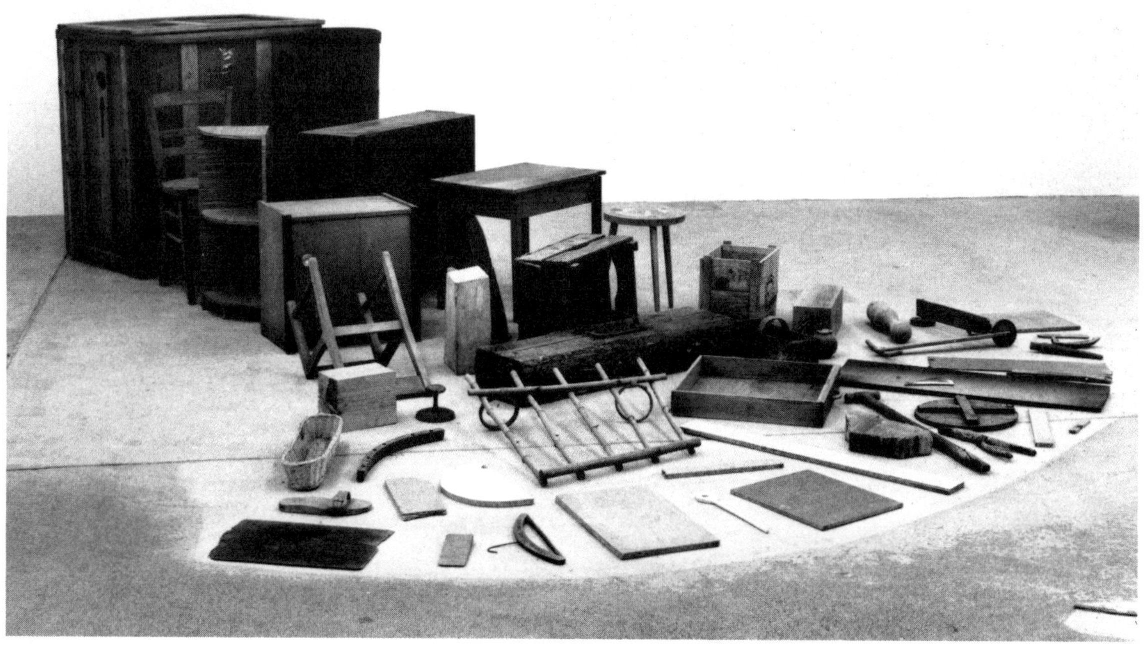

One sculpture from a three part installation at Documenta 7 in Kassel, *Large Axe Head 1982* (collection: Tate Gallery, London), was made in wood. The other elements were Boat (metal objects) and Horn (blue objects).

Cragg's wall installations in plastic. *Yellow Fragment 1980* (collection: Dr Franklin) opened an epoch where the material had a less provocative role and became a vehicle for making images, a personal drawing method. Materials and objects became subordinate to the images.

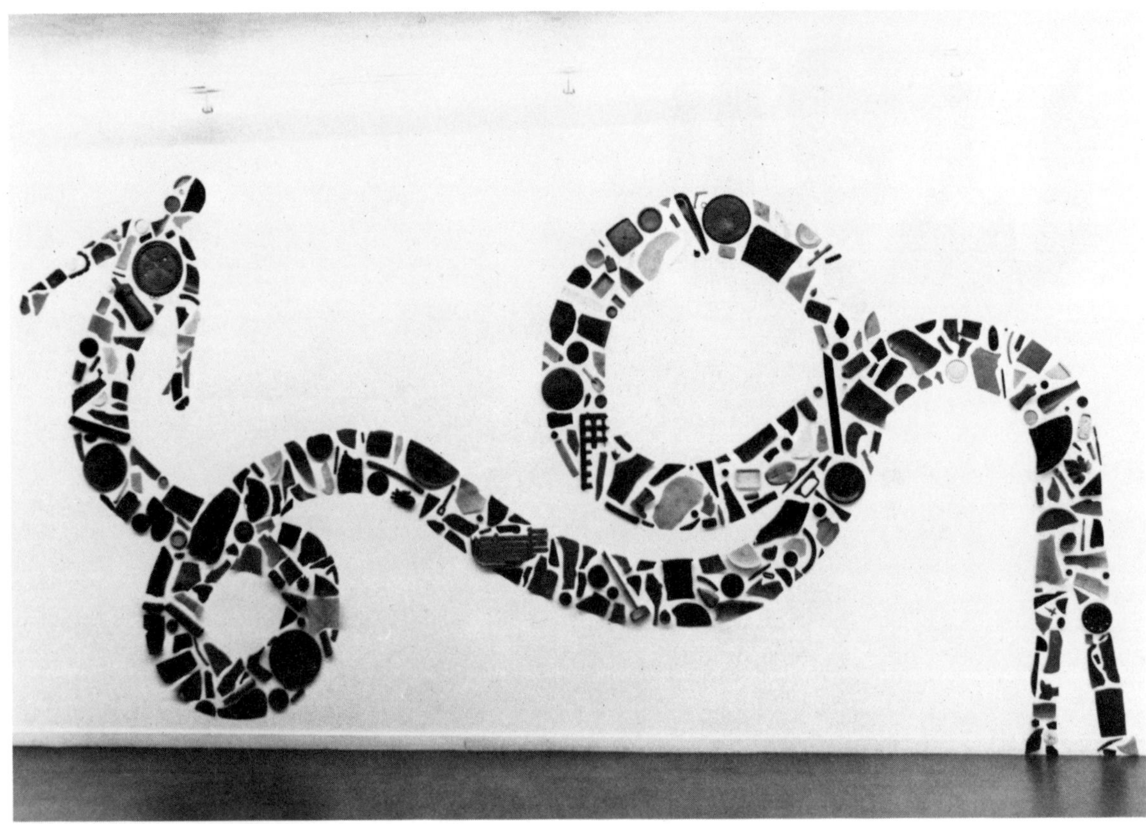

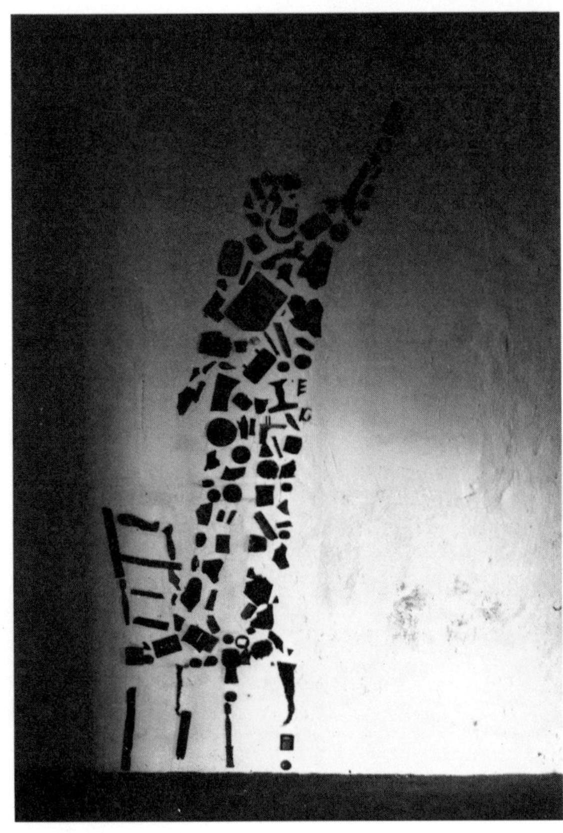

Self Portrait on Chair 1980 (collection: Thomas Cohn).

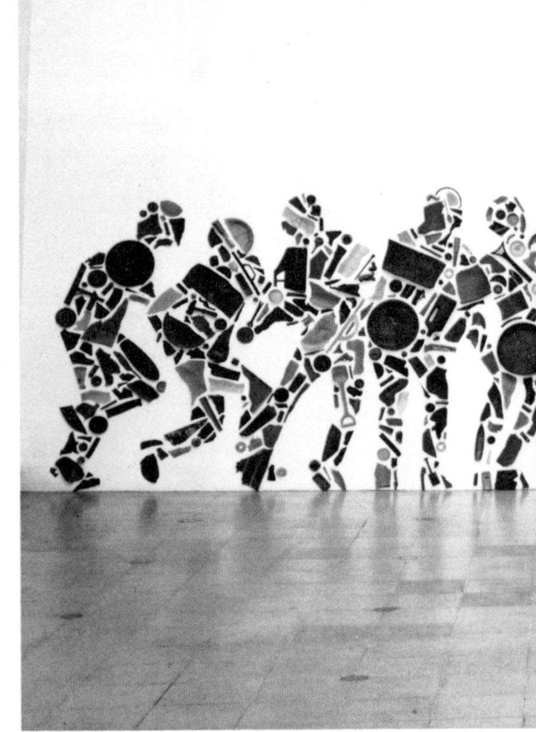

Riot 1986 (collection: Saatchi, London).

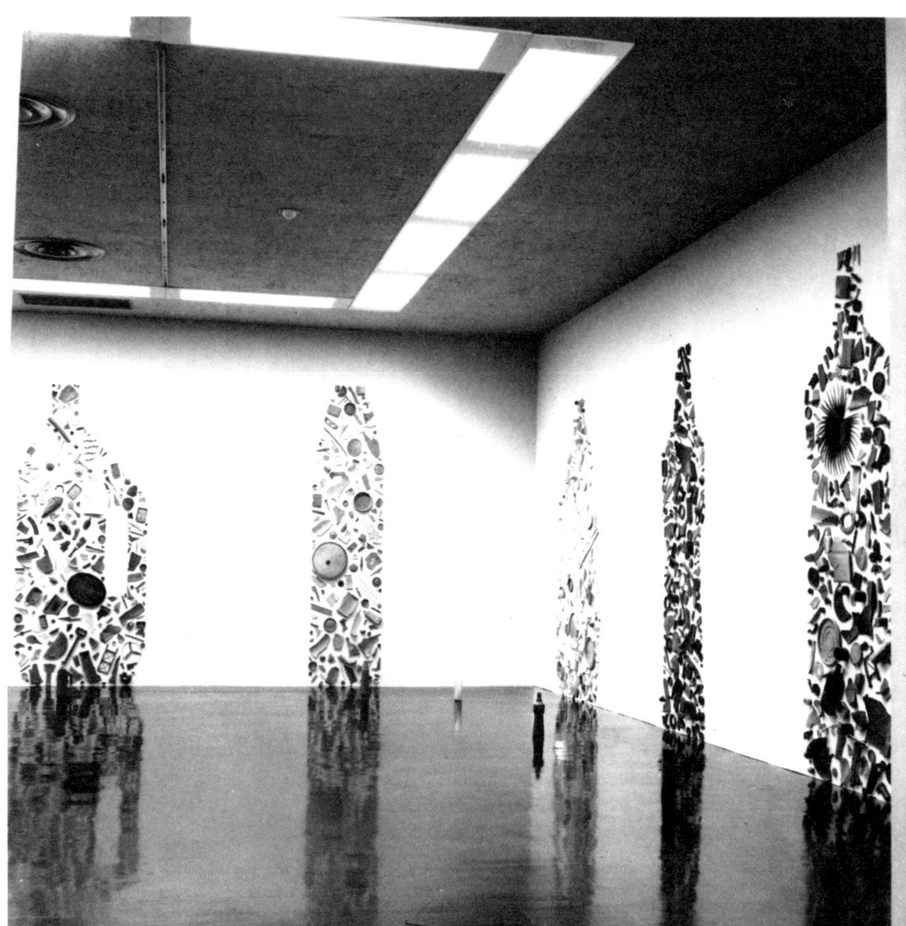

Five Bottles 1982.

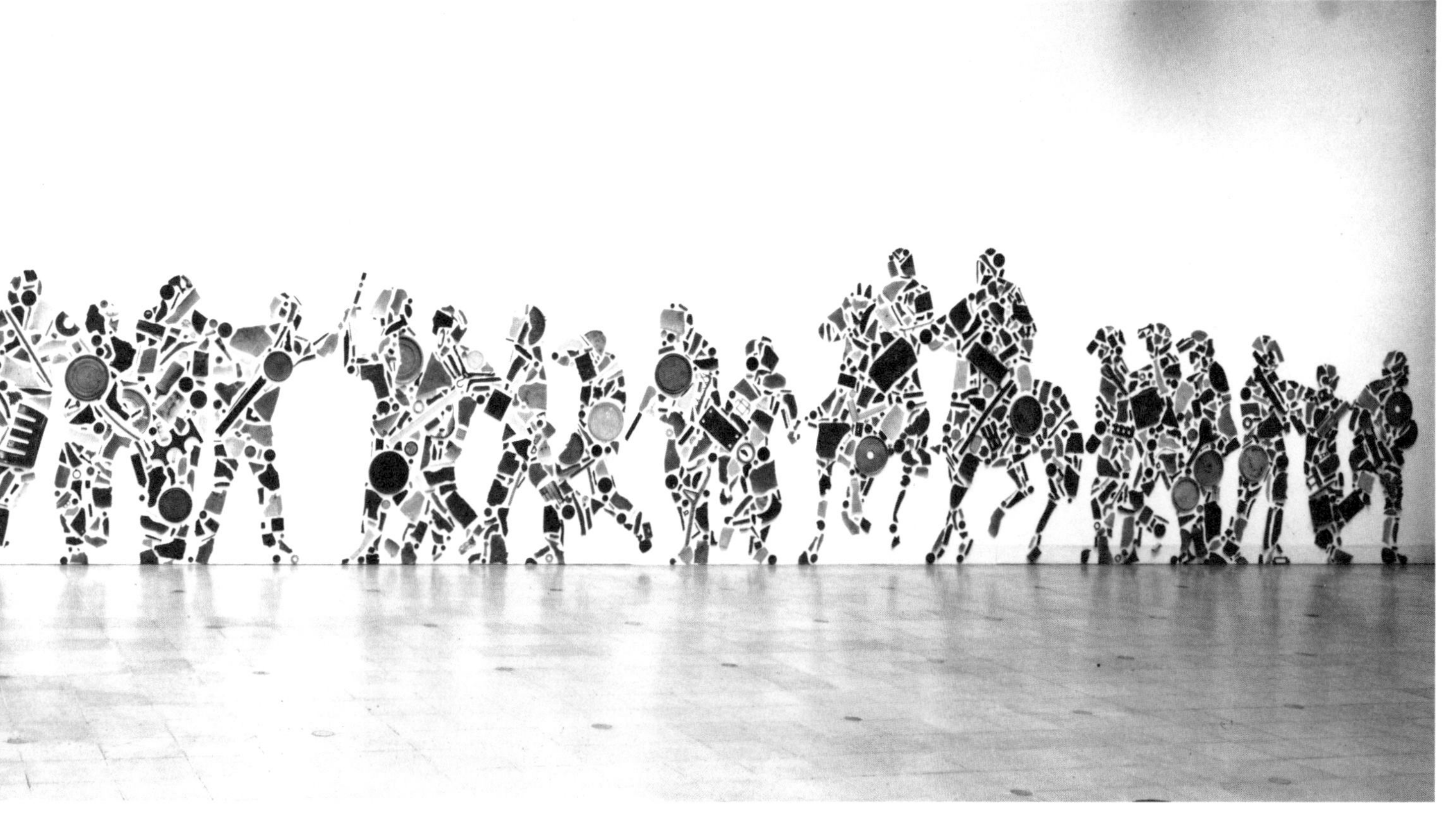

At the Konrad
Fischer Gallery in
Dusseldorf, an
installation with
*House and Trough
1982,* in diverse black
and white materials
and *Mercedes 1982,*
the emblem of the
motor-car, made in
street riot materials;
bricks and bottles.

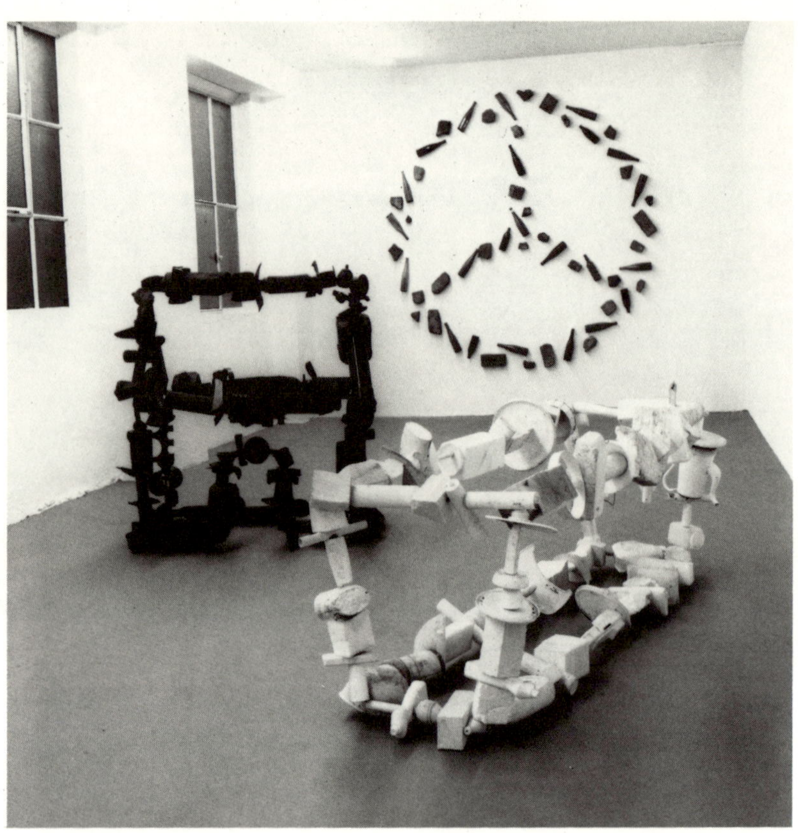

Man made objects
combined with na-
tural materials in a
precarious constell-
ation, underlines an
ever-recurring pre-
occupation with the
relationship between
a *designed* world and
a *natural* world. *Two
Tables and Four
Stones 1983*
(courtesy: Bernd
Klüser Gallery,
Munich) was exhi-
bited at Cragg's one
man show at the
Kunsthalle, Berne.

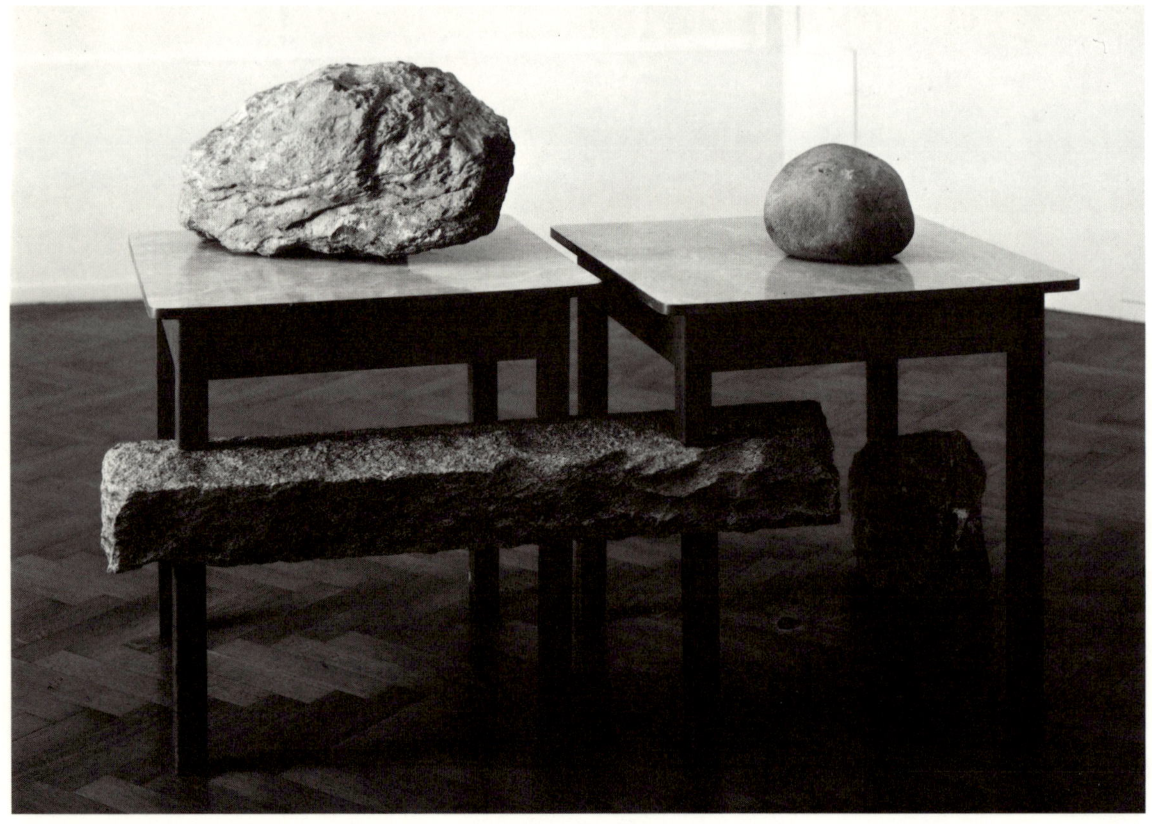

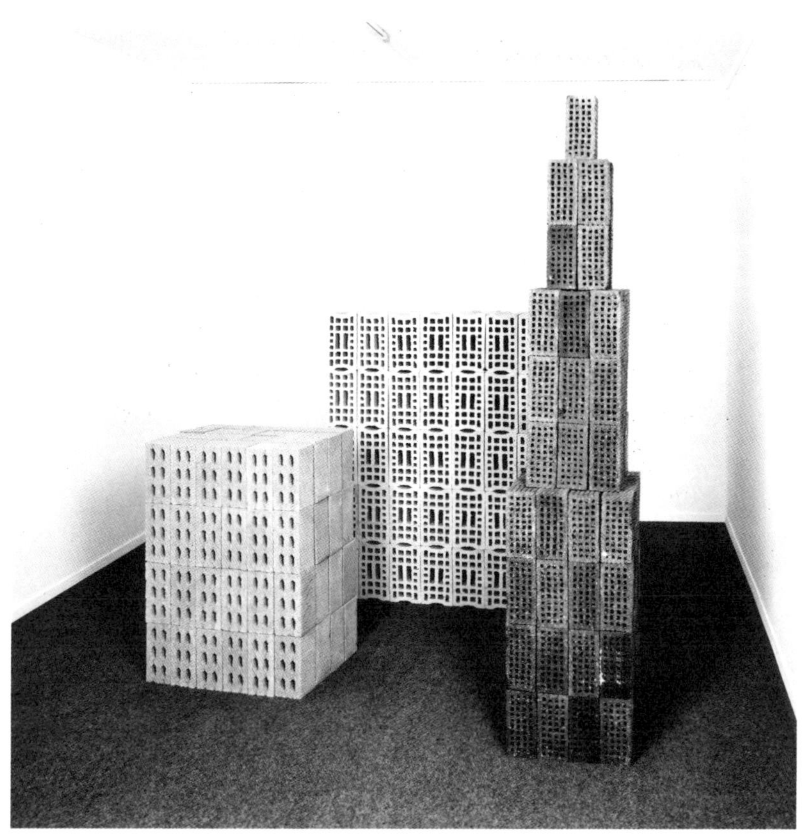

At Galerie Buchmann, *Three Modern Buildings 1983* (private collection, Cologne).

At Toselli, Milan, *Large Mountain 1983* (courtesy: Galeria Toselli).

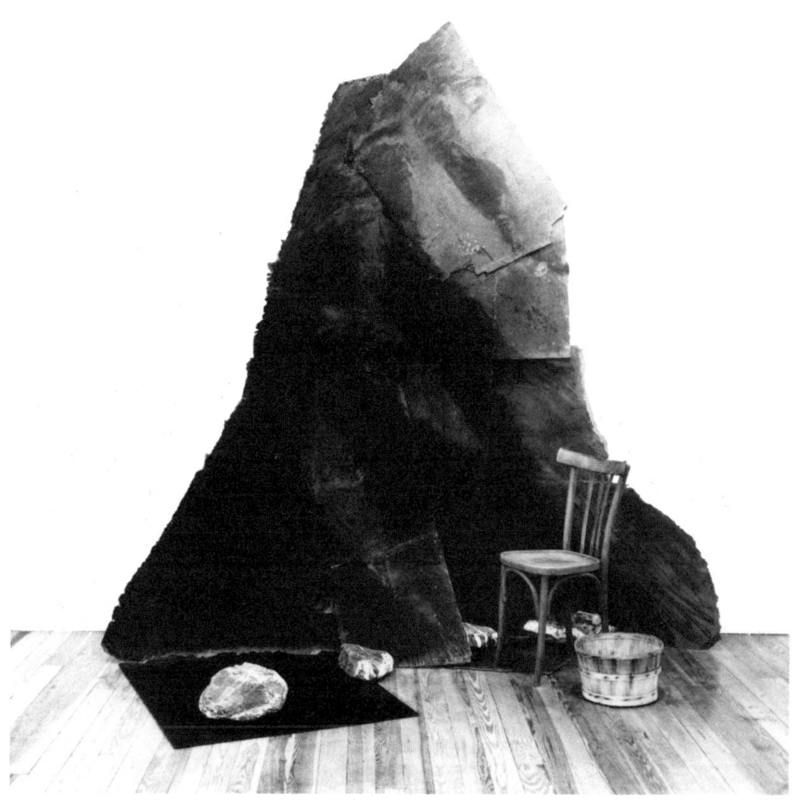

Echo 1984 is a large landscape, based on the memory of a journey between Lille and Turin, driving over Mont Blanc.

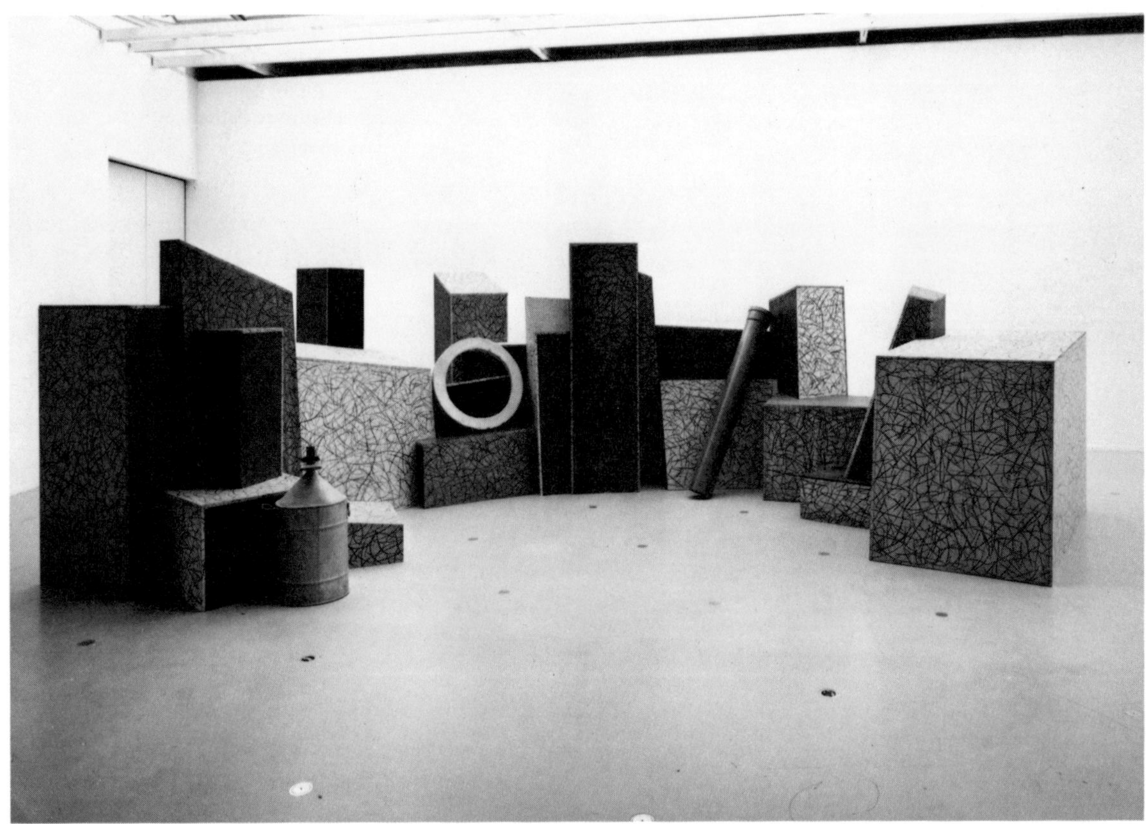

George and the Dragon 1984 (collection: Arts Council of Great Britain).

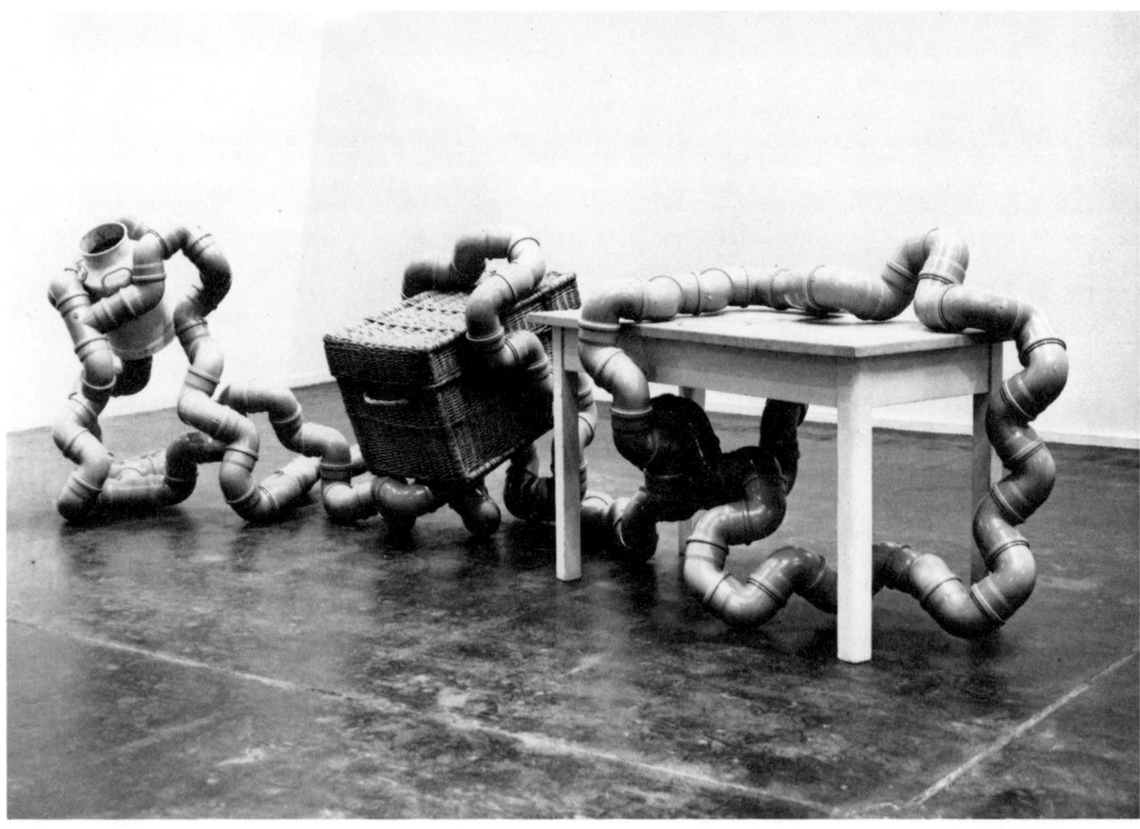

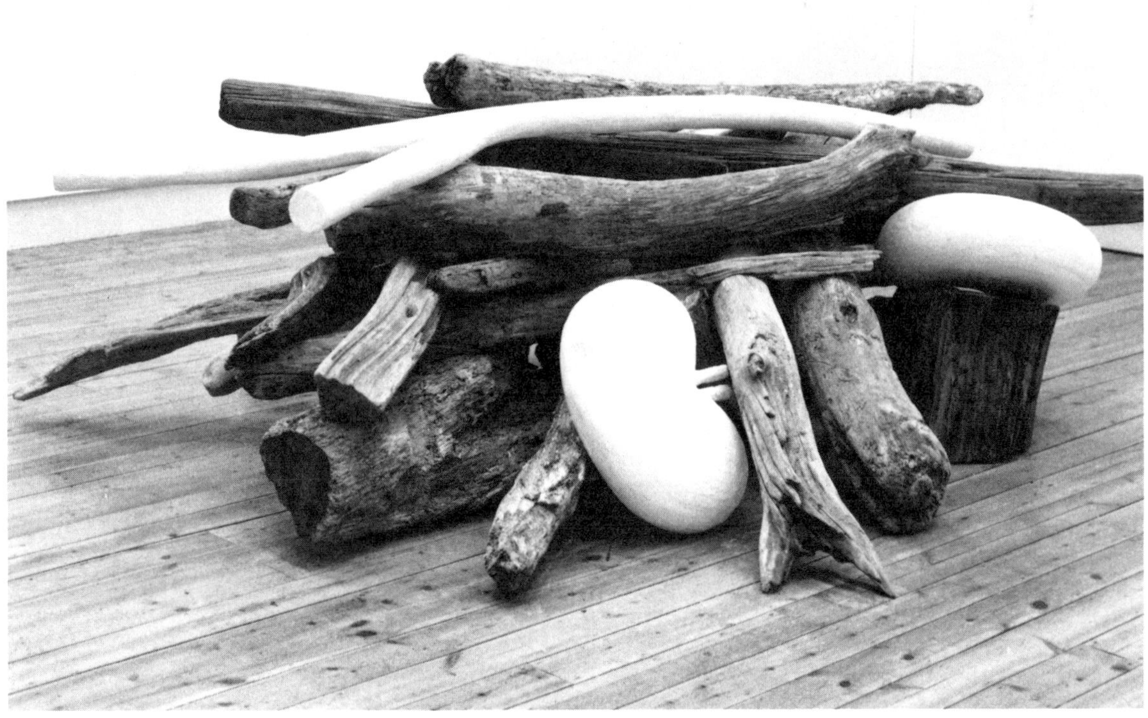

Wooden Muscle 1986.

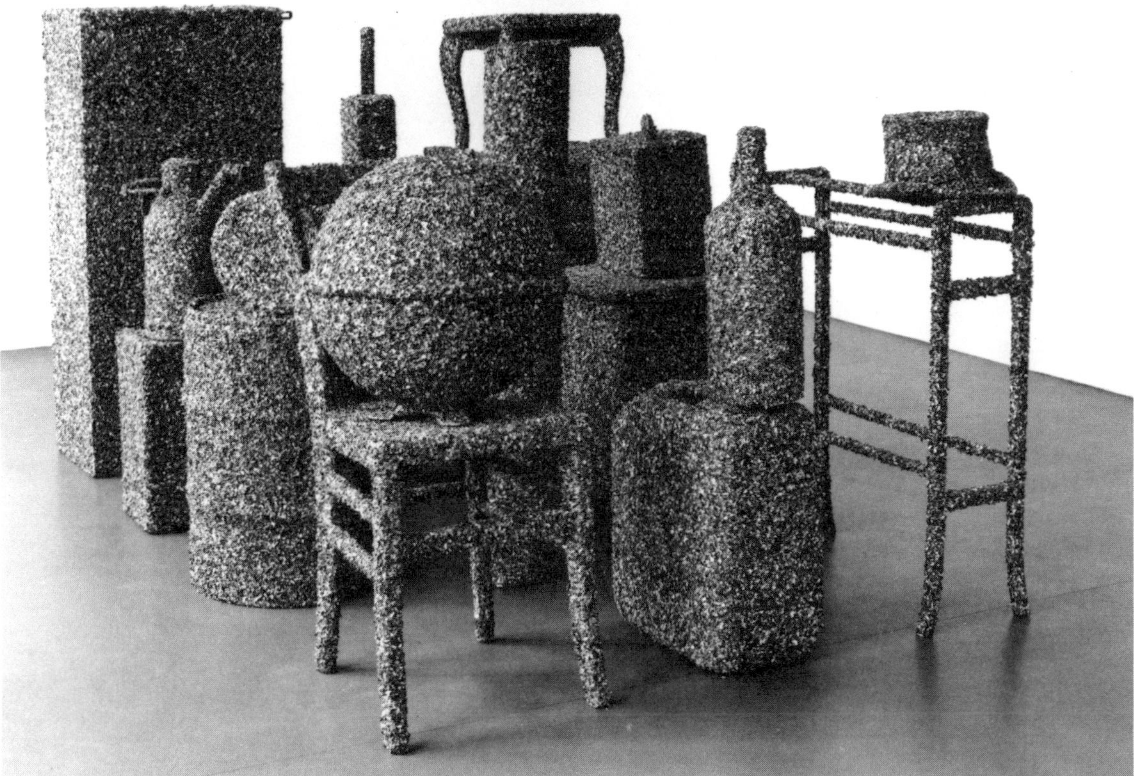

Advancing every day objects camouflaged with a layer of plastic chips, *Birnam Wood 1985*.
(collection: Eyck).

Exhibition in the
Konrad Fischer
Gallery
Eye Bath 1986
(collection: Saatchi,
London),
Float 1986,
Mortar and Pestle
1986.

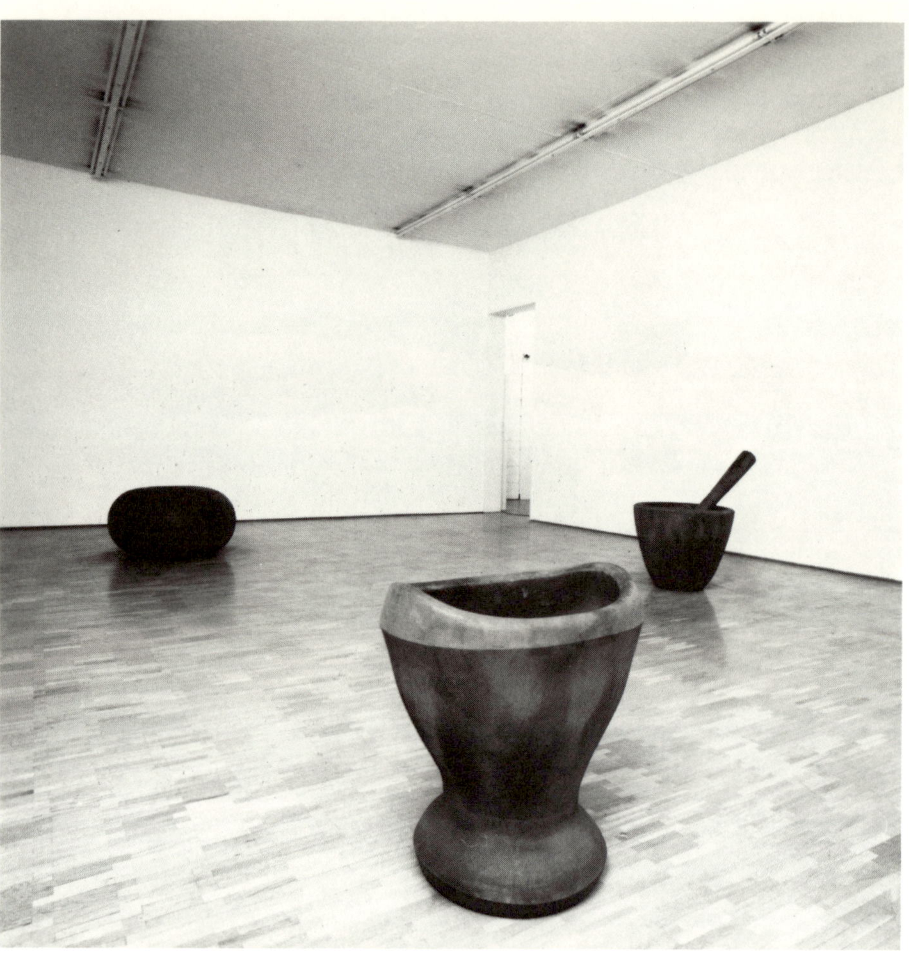

Radio Shacks 1986
(private collection,
Berne).

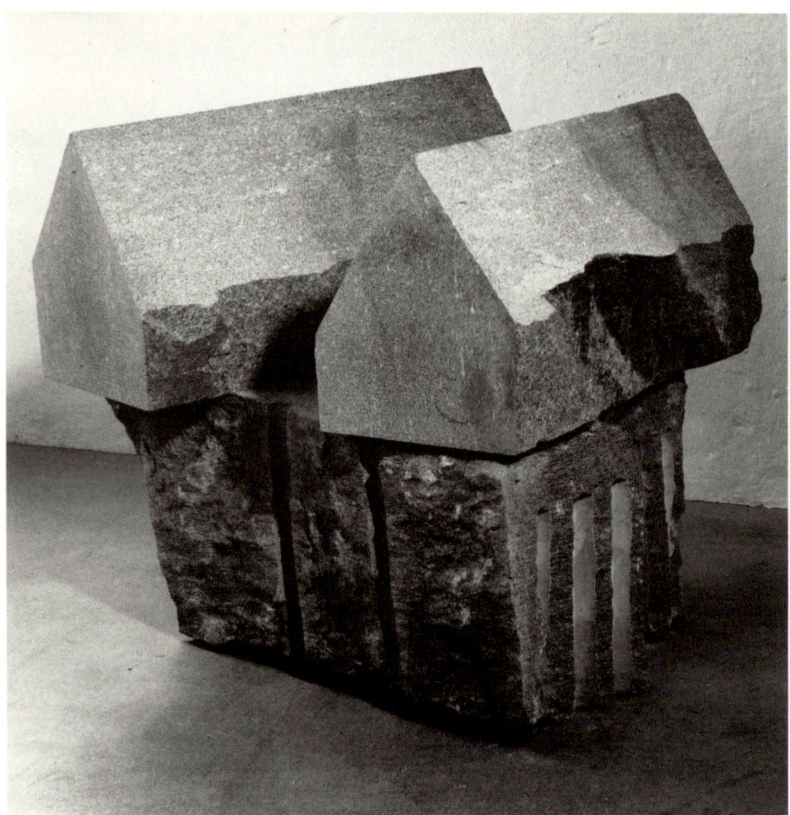

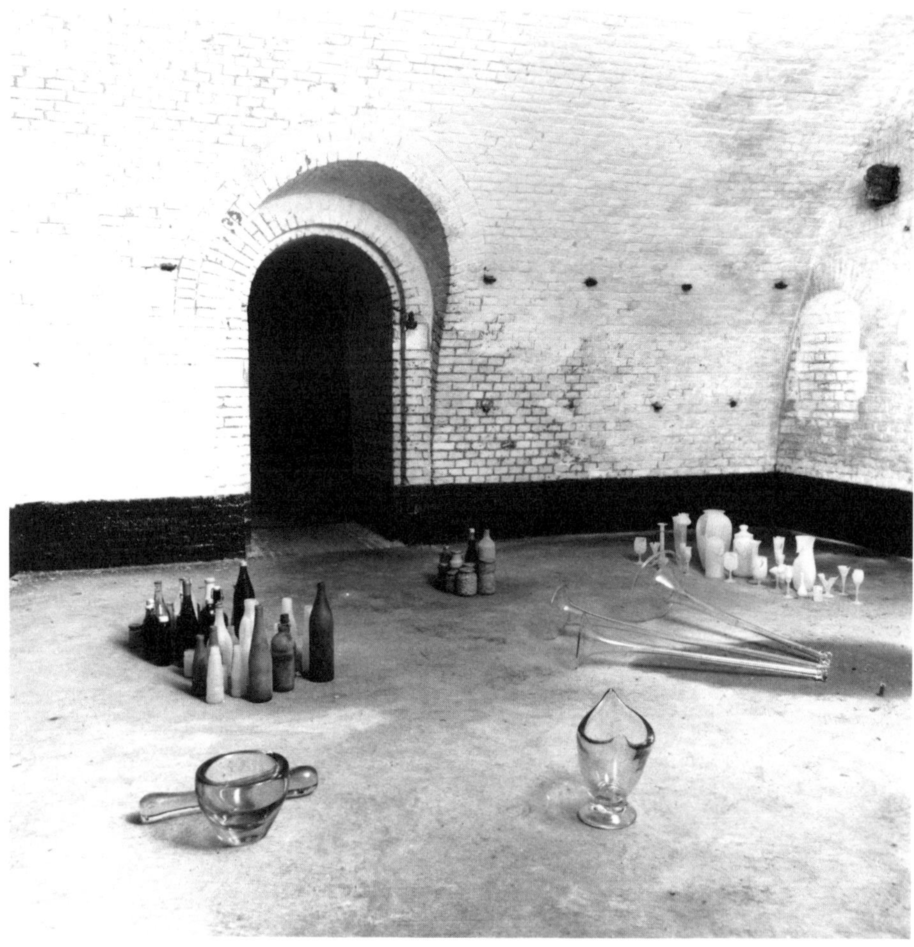

An installation view at Fort Asperen 1986. *Mortar and Pestle, Eye Bath, Glass Horns, Sand Blasted Glass, and Commercial Food Containers with their Original Contents.*

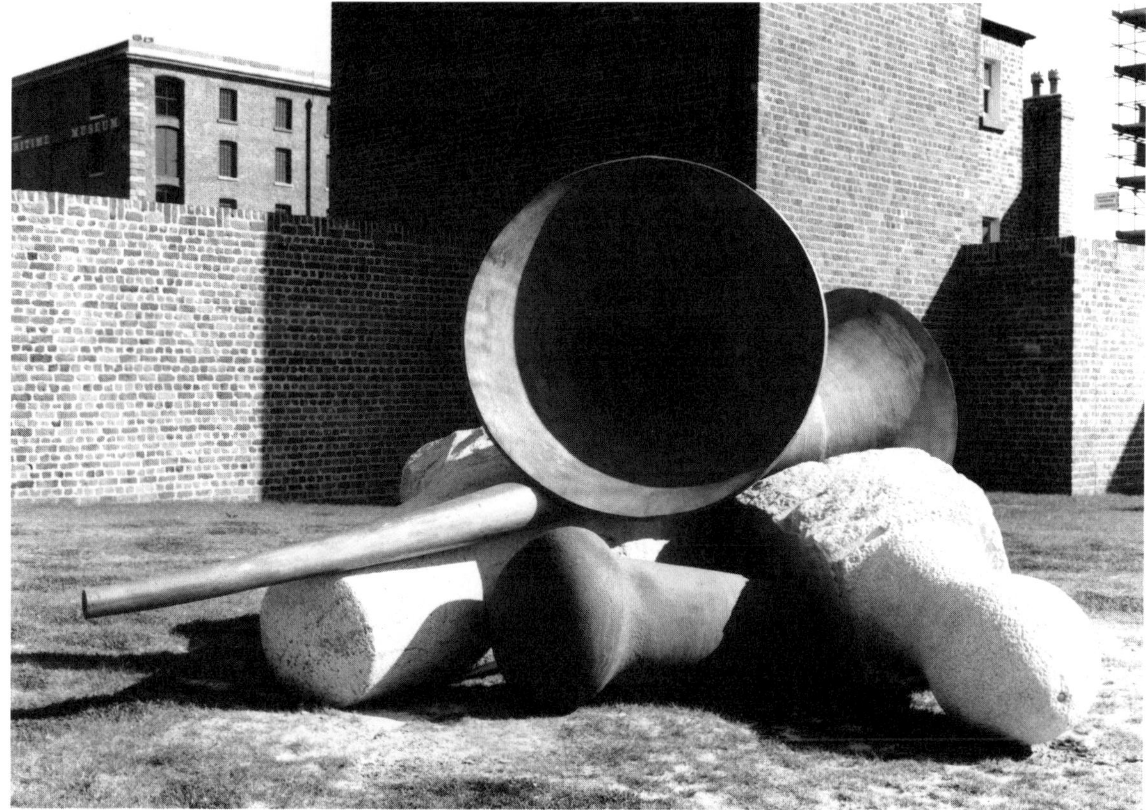

Raleigh 1986 (collection: Tate Gallery).

Tools 1986
(collection: Saatchi,
London).

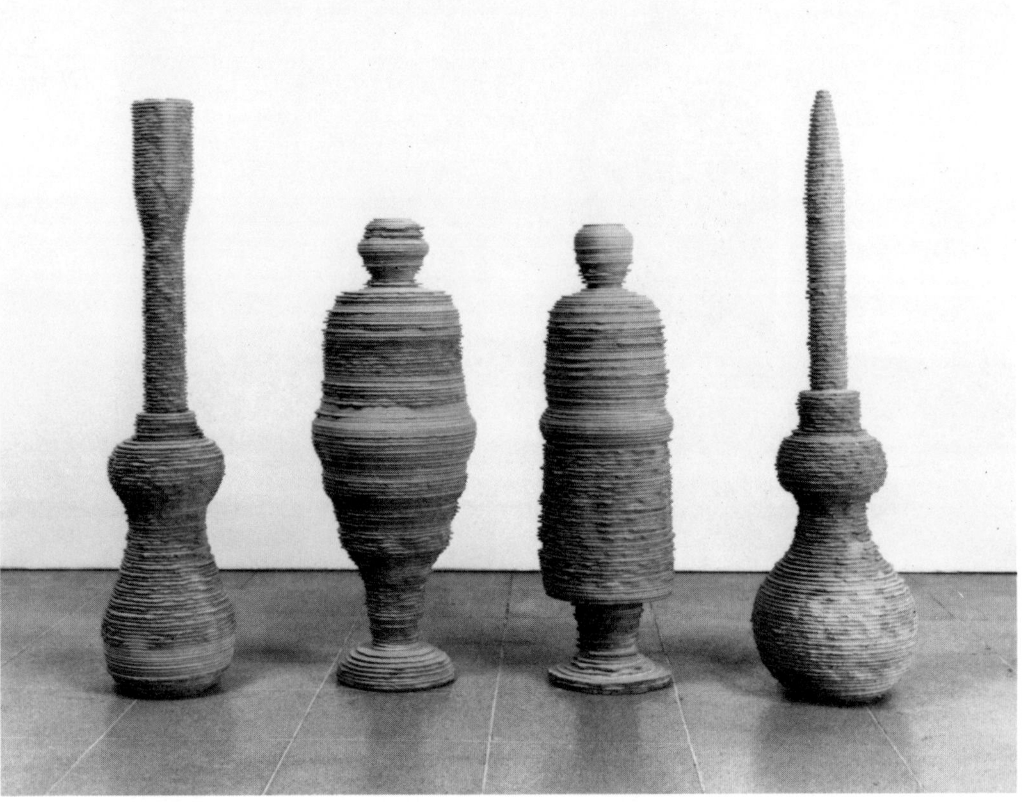

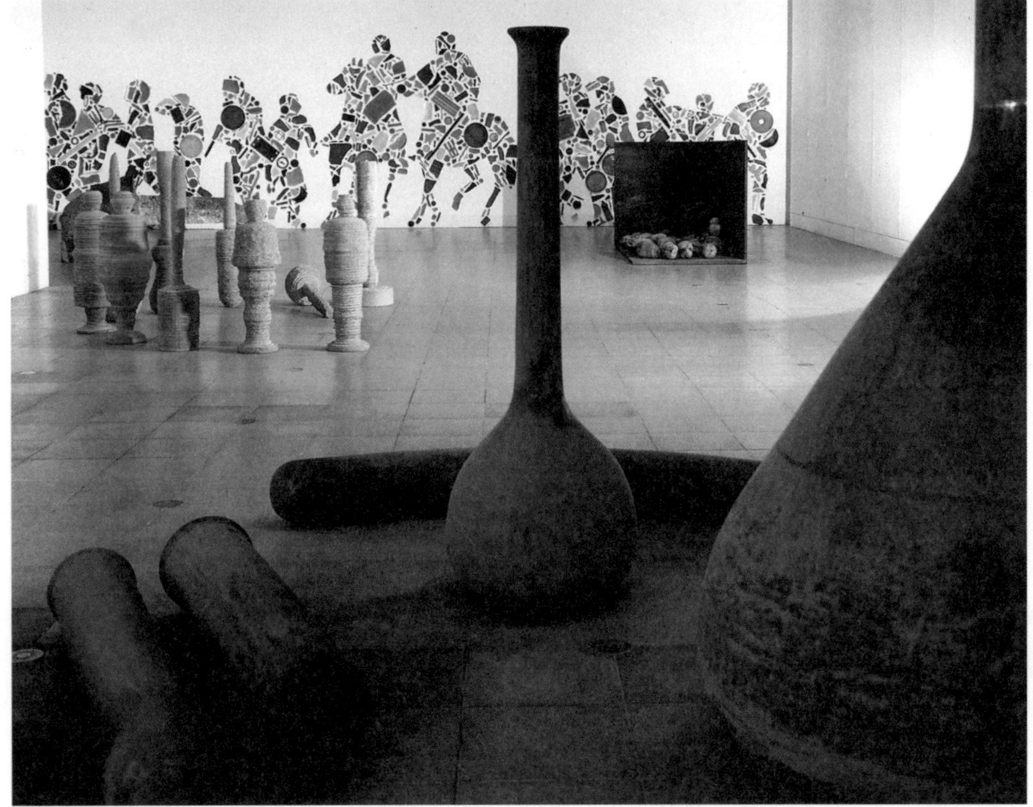

Hayward Gallery,
London,
Exhibition 1987
showing, front to
back
*Contained Reactions
1987*
(collection: Saatchi,
London),
Tools 1986
(collection: Saatchi,
London),
*Hassocks and
Keymer 1986*
(collection: Saatchi,
London),
*Inverted Sugar Crop
1986*
(collection: Saatchi,
London),
Riot 1987
(collection: Saatchi,
London).

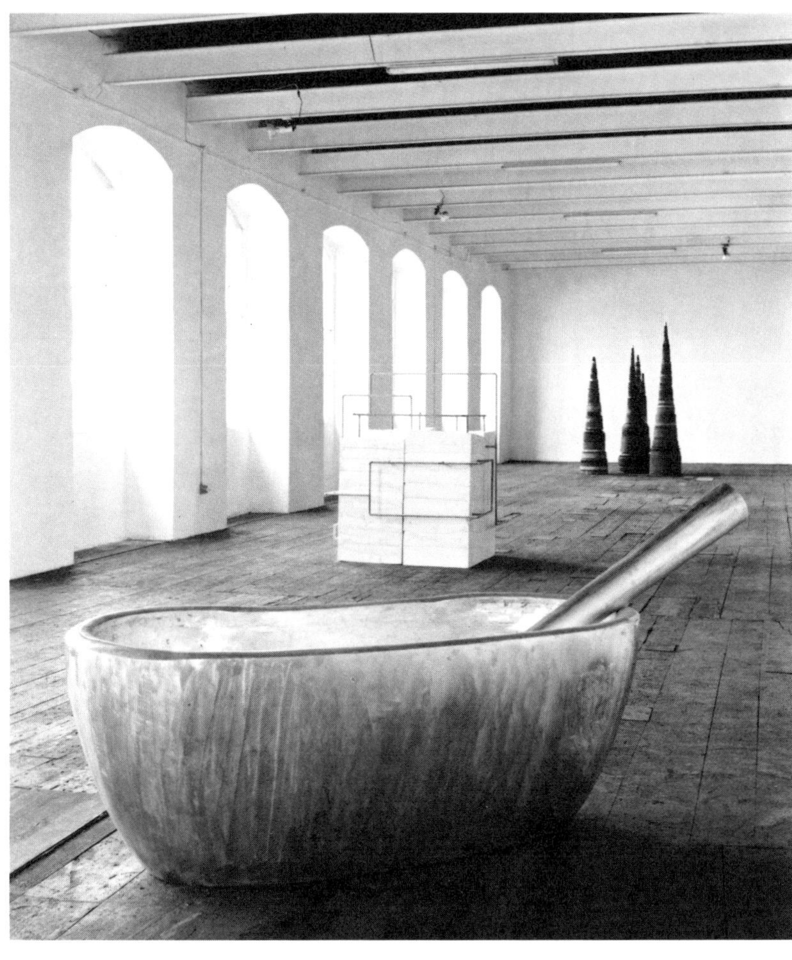

Galleria Tucci Russo,
Turin, Exhibition
1987
showing front to
back
*Mortar and Pestle
1987*
(private collection
Turin)
Calcium Strata 1987
Guglie 1987
(collection: Lisa and
Tucci Russo).

Documenta 8. In an
exhibition dedicated
to the glorification
of the found &
designed object.
Provisional title.
Earth Product 1987
(collection: Hayman)
opposed this
attitude.

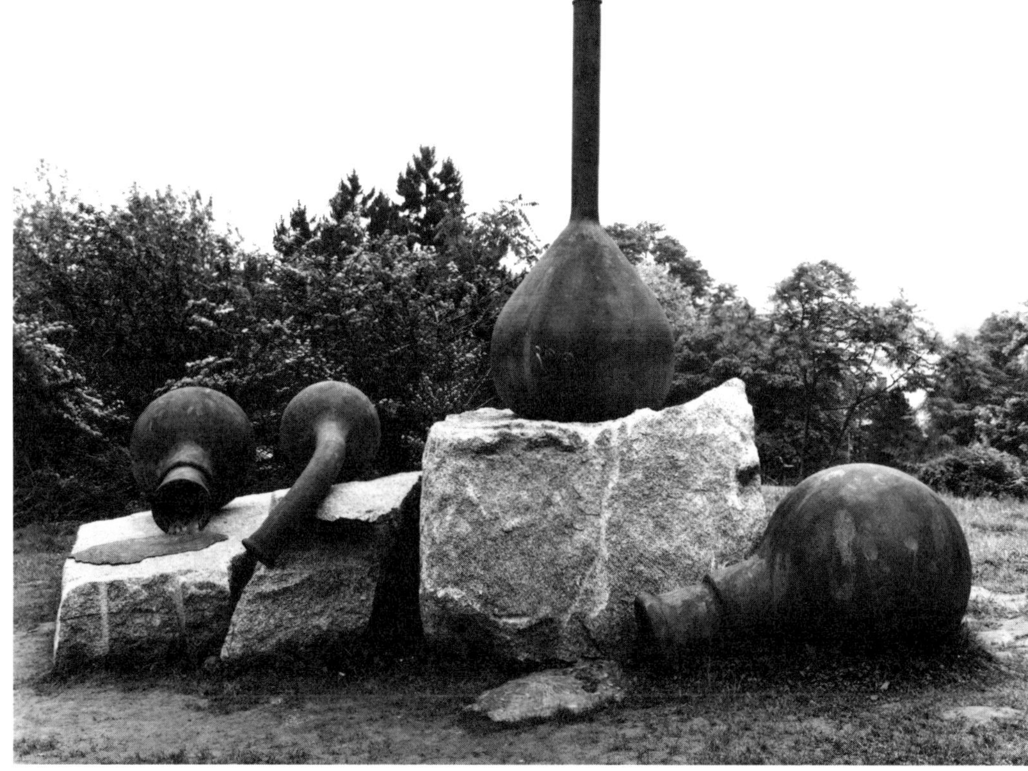

Tony Cragg

Tony Cragg is preoccupied by a crusading theme which will very likely last a lifetime. As he delves into it, aspects more tantalising and more foreboding arise. His theme commits him to the studio and gallery because he sees these as two of the few remaining places where people can hope to exercise the faculties of seeing, feeling and thinking in order to create options which can run counter to the brutal tide of the manufactured world's criteria. To begin with, every sculpture should puncture and overwhelm our natural passivity. From that advantage, the 'useless' objects are suffused with mystery and form, equivalent to phenomena existing in the disappearing natural world. If this sequence already sounds decidedly grandiose, in fact Cragg expects more of his sculptures. They should open themselves, after scrutiny, to interpretations that are literary, metaphoric, erotic, spiritual, poetic and not least metaphysical. The meanings extracted by individuals are not like correct answers, nor are they conveniently lodged at 'multi-levels' (a pallative disclaimer Cragg finds meaningless). Quixotically, in order to succeed, the sculptures themselves should normally look untrammelled and lucid and constitute a population that can travel.

In three previous catalogues for one-person exhibitions in Brussels, Hanover and London, Cragg provided interviews and conversation-enriched texts. The propositions are remarkably consistent (as no doubt will be his voice within this publication). Cragg stated to Demosthenes Davvetas who was interviewing him in 1985, 'These last years I have been working over a thematical area and set of interests which includes the ever increasing gap that exists between the visible world and the information world which is rapidly growing larger and larger. Man functions in everyday life without knowing what the objects around him are, he is hardly aware of the political situation, the social reality, the chemical problems, and even basic things like what electricity is. People are constantly talking about progress, yet they seem to forget that the progress they are talking about is only material, whereas man himself, his basic condition, hardly evolves. I am looking for associations, images and symbols which could enrich and enlarge my vocabulary of responses to the world I see and even function as thinking models.'[1]

Cragg amplified the comments in the published conversation with Lynne Cooke in 1987; 'If we're making a mess of things, like polluting the world, that's relatively simple to stop; it's something else that concerns me more. That is, to live in a world that has become predominantly artificial and man-made. That I can accept as long as the man-made world is providing images and meanings which are just as deep and meaningful as those which are found with naturally ocurring things. ... If one wants to hear the radio in preference to bird-song, if it has values that one can accept, fine, but I think then one has really to develop its potential.'[2]

Several assumptions recur in each instalment of Cragg's testament which indicate the extent of his evangelistic expectations. All could alarm the reader. The first suggests that one's surroundings become more gratifying and stimulating if one has mastered the fundamentals of physics and chemistry. Most people, especially those who frequent museums, are practical up to the level of a boy-scout, and, if stranded on a resources-rich but deserted island, would find it impossible to recall their secondary education and create electricity much less motorcars, television and computers. Many flagrant demonstrations of knowledge of the arts and nature are paired with a boastful ignorance of science. Cragg does not have this point of view or limitation. Although he practised in a scientific field for only two years, as a 17–19 year-old laboratory technician, he continues learning about genetics, chemistry, engineering, and more. He has a need to understand and applies educated consideration when debating whether to purchase a halogen or tungsten lamp or a particular brand of video camera, or painting acid on a sculpture.

The second place where Cragg's art makes us feel insecure is his devotion to the idea of banal objects being as potentially informative and as rich in aesthetic and emotional spin-offs as traditional art, figurative or abstract. We look at his sculpture and ask ourselves, does he especially like what it was modelled upon, this one particular plastic bottle? Has he stumbled upon something with stylistic grace, like Picasso's racing bicycle seat and handlebars which previous to and after being 'cited' by an artist stood as visually magnificent? Or is his enlargement just another version of the current, rather shallow, appropriation and glorification of the faceless output of mass-production? Take Cragg's *Three Modern Buildings*. In its several versions the tiered stacks, all composed of porous, synthetic thermalite, imitated Manhattan skyscrapers. Standing on the sculpture court at the Hayward Gallery in 1987 facing the Shell Building they looked decidedly like the window-dominated chunks of prefabricated office and apartment blocks put up to replace war-ravaged and decayed structures in towns throughout Northern Europe. They strike one as dispiriting. The uglier one's environment the more excuse to concentrate on gratification of one's vanity within a closed circle of taste. However, Cragg's sensibility intervened and somehow the pink, grey/yellow reflected light of London's river front transformed the material, as it did with the companion towers of *Minster*. One then thinks that with more attention perhaps a modern city could become memorable by way of subtle landmarks which stir and enrich our minds.

We cannot answer the question of what Cragg cherishes; the artist's accessible point is that responsibility is individual, not a matter of taste. Prince Charles tells a Pittsburgh audience in March 1988 of the successful rejuvenation of an old textile mill in Halifax for present-day uses, and suggests that when architects build from scratch they should 'encourage the renaissance of craftsmanship and the art of embellishing buildings for man's pleasure and for the sheer joy in beauty itself, as opposed to mere functionalism'.[3] Cragg himself covets occupying a Jugendstil factory with leaded windows adjacent to his studio in the Wichlinghausen area of Wuppertal, the first European city

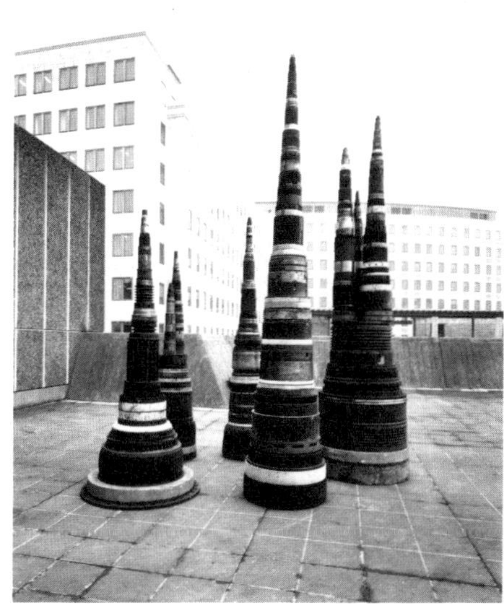

Minster 1987 (Collection: Saatchi, London).

to be industrialised. Heavily bombed, it is now a contrast of handsome pre-war mansions and noble factories and eyesores. Neither Cragg nor the Prince believes it is simply the designers and architects who have poisoned our environment. Cragg seems to impute the blame to all devotees of the consumer society, politicians included, who although long past actually being hungry or over-crowded, blind themselves to the quiet, effervescent, poetic meanings left in our man-scarred natural world and smother their curiosity as well as their sensory responses.

Cragg promotes again and again the simple idea of really looking, and from visual specu-lation, deriving empathy and poetry. If, for example, the starting point is a row of bottles on top of his refrigerator, he describes a 250ml mineral water bottle as dumpy, noting that its swelling shoulder allows the bubbles to condense without exploding, and the profile left by the mould is imperfect. On the other hand, the Gordon's gin bottle has square military shoulders and clear glass to enhance the idea of gin's potency and anaesthetising effect, and gives the illusion of volume. Anyone who goes back to the studio with a similarly stringent outlook and who takes the trouble to look, will also be dissatisfied with the gimcrack, anachronistic type of post-modernist design. Cragg reminds us that some of the most astonishing twentieth century inventions are based on simple binary electrical principles; thus all that was required was ordinary human comprehension made extraordinary by concentration.

One Cragg-like way to break new ground is to forge ahead without any pre-conceived method or diplomacy, the mind fixated on a mirage with the desired ambiance and moral factor. *Plough* began this way. Cragg intended his sculpture to reserve the tool's function of masticating the earth while itself remaining unscathed. After persuading a farmer to sell his old, rusting plough standing in a field, the artist reproduced each part in wax. The surrogate plough was then softened by the heat of a hair dryer until he could sink his teeth into a few of the bars. The elements were cast in steel and the plough reconstructed. Nothing about this sequence was intentionally clever. 'Looking for solutions, provides new answers', is his explanation, as if to say that the ingenious parts are thrown in for free.

In early March 1988 the plough stood near the mazzanine office area of the perfectly daylit studio, formerly a textile factory. In other parts lay the materials of former works — metal, rubber and wood circles for the minsters, boxes of scavanged plastic, several plastic chip-coated objects including a bicycle pushed together, plaster moulds and a set of the wooden-block forms used in the manufacture of a steam engine. In progress as possibly Venice-bound work there was a polystyrene enlargement of the fossil called a 'Devil's toenail', a three-part still-life modelled on three plastic objects, and more. If you wander around this warehouse, it becomes clear that the earlier idea of Cragg as one of the last artists to nominate a new material was only correct in so far as it went. Scavanged plastic did follow the soup can, light bulb, bricks, and stones in the Andes; the sequence and conceptual simplicity gave the young artist much of his inspiration. Now, however, he is running several sub-themes all tangential to the physical sciences and allowing them to accumulate until there is a suggestion of a grand design with powerful erotic and emotional substance. The studio carries an atmosphere of inculcating the world with art. Much of the multi-stage, large-scale making has to be done in partnership with assistants, a number of them artists, in addition to stone masons, carpenters and foundry workers. The impressive thing is that Cragg is not just running a financially demanding, highly motivated studio to keep pace with his fecundity of ideas; Cragg has to set goals more formidable than the imminence of the next exhibition. Scanning the lists in his sketchbooks, made for just this purpose, one finds many objects in generic code; thus geo-model, eaten landscape, extended chemistry bottles or first volumes. Others are named by source like eye-bath and a few are romantic, even documentary titles like 'Birnam Wood' or a series, yet to appear, 'shipwreck'.

The categories and references link. The mineral resources of the earth, water and sun are seen as sustaining the animal kingdom, such that we people are eating earth. The 'landscape' sculptures *Inverted Sugar Crop, Plough, Wooden Muscle, Jurassic Landscape* and the new *Alpine Landscape* introduce metaphors both sinister and poignant. Cragg quotes Guthrie, 'I saw Adam leave the garden / With an apple in his hand. / What are you going to do? / Plant a bit of grain, he said; / Pray for a bit of rain, he said. / There ain't much time / And we're only passing thru.'[4] The earth reclaims us. The body is a microcosm and so is sculpture. It follows that the conversion of organic matter to energy which goes on in the organs and tissue is artistically a matter of scale, volume and layering. *Spleen* and *Capillular landscape* are examples. The chain of associations continues with the organ-like implements, flasks and test tubes belonging to the chemist. When they are transformed by a studio sand-blasting machine, they conjure up the glass bottles found on the shore, wonderfully eroded, not smashed, by the waves.

Philosophic or poetic inroads can begin anywhere. The manufacturers of the giant washing-up liquid bottle, profit-eager and attuned to labour-saving detail, elected a smooth moulded design with an inbuilt handle, thus creating a large ovoid of negative space. Cragg no more than any well-educated sculptor can ignore the tradition of negative space having the power of mass and the metaphor of loss. This simple fact remained strange and seductive to Henry Moore; erosion in hillsides and cliffs were as direct images of mortality as the organic ones that haunted him, the eye-sockets in a skull and bullet-holes tunnelling through flesh. The alarming chasm at the neck of the enormous Cragg sculpture (*Bestükkung*) accords with the uncomfortable way objects modelled on plastic trivia are welded to the sides. The image expresses the Lilliputian horror of little creatures clinging to a featureless cliff face. Cragg sees them as a visualisation of the

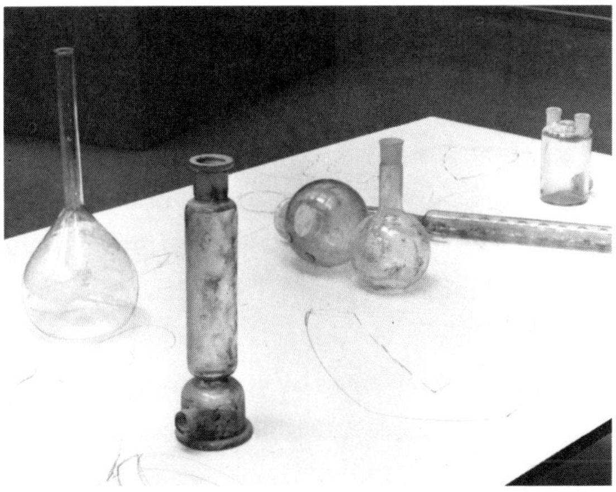

Project for: *Im Auftrag* (Folkwang, Essen).

antibodies that attach to cells. And from there he conjures the image of the dreaded HIV antibodies perhaps dormant in our bloodstream.

Something rather pedantic and driven would attach to an art which insisted we should be forced to look at the banal objects on the supermarket shelves and motorways in order to force ourselves to find meaning in our lives. This could be wearisome. Joseph Beuys was inevitably an influence, though officially expelled from the Kunstakademie, Düsseldorf, by the time Cragg himself began teaching there in 1979. Beuys' proclamation, 'Every human being is an artist' and warnings like, 'Environmental pollution advances parallel with a pollution of the world within us' were liberating messages as much as ones filled with doom.[5] The call for communal action, however, failed to sustain Cragg's sense of mission. Befittingly, as he gets older, he identifies impulsively with the creative side of the great, reclusive scientists. He sees their minds as intent on discovery while their instincts are attracted to the scent given by the dark and fantastical side of investigation.

One of Cragg's personal heroes is Isaac Newton. Something that impressed him in Richard Westfall's definitive biography and scientific appreciation is that Newton 'observed the shadows in every room he frequented and, if asked, would look at the shadow instead of the clock to give the time'.[6] Cragg trains his nerves and reactions to be that finely calibrated. The self-portraits in plastic are of his shadow, hunched and severe, or his profile, spun 360 degrees. Cragg points out that alchemy was a consuming passion for Newton in contradiction to the fact that one of his great achievements was to rationalise chemistry so profoundly that it could at last contribute to the laws of natural philosophy. Alchemists in the 17th century, according to Westfall, 'believed that life rather than mechanism stands at the very heart of nature. All things are generated by the conjunction of male and female: metals differ in no wise from the rest of nature', indeed gold is merely 'the product that nature realises when nothing interrupts her normal gestation.'[7] For Newton, the most mesmerising factor was the spirit, it was at the base root of everything, rising up from the earth, through our heads to the atmosphere and the sun and stars. Without the spirit, matter, even gold, was vulgar.

The touching and prophetic description by the twenty year-old Mary Shelley of the young scientist Frankenstein stresses his ardent desire to create a species that could beget descendents; 'No father could claim the gratitude of his child so completely as I should deserve theirs.'[8] In sight of bringing life to his fiend he remembers experiencing heightened sensual powers; 'Although I possessed the capacity of bestowing animation, yet to prepare a frame for the reception of it, with all its intricacies of fibres, muscles, and veins, still remained a work of inconceivable difficulty and labour. I prepared myself for a multitude of reverses; my operations might be incessantly baffled.'[9] Indeed the struggle stretches into the winter before he draws near to succeeding, 'But my enthusiasm was checked by my anxiety, and I appeared rather like one doomed by slavery to toil in the mines, or any other unwholesome trade than an artist occupied by his favourite employment.'[10]

Cragg, like all artists wants his art at least metaphorically to come to life, if only to become one's own surrogate companion. The megalomaniacal side is inseparable from the erotic one. Cragg believes, 'Freedom is becoming less and less and what freedom we do have is basically between our ears. To improve the quality of what's between one's ears, and I do mean quality not just quantity, one can make an erotic response to the external world.' Cragg is indifferent to titillating, stereotyped erotic imagery. He proposes that if one looks hard enough at the salt and pepper cellars on the table, their erotic potential will surface since our chain of associations in that hypnotic state is so unstoppable. Desire makes us become specialists. For instance, the feelings contained in a facial expression register with everyone; to someone obsessed by form they can transfer to the perception of a concave/convex shift, or projection, or point of contact between two objects. When Cragg describes a sculpture's length, he says 'from me to you'. The rim of the enlarged eyebath he made in 1986 is engorged; the matching mortar and pestle convey a sexual metaphor without exploiting any kind of gestural reaction.

The references to coupling and reproduction are hardly unqualified joyous expressions of the life cycle. Lurking under the mammoth 'Devil's toenail' fossil are several musical instrument cases. It soon becomes apparent that their original function to protect wind instruments which, in turn, are evolved versions of the natural conch shell, indicates the questionable superiority of man-induced evolution. The large form is either giving birth to or ravaging the little ones; the parent who begets and nourishes has also the latent instinct to devour his offspring who are, after all, on earth to replace him. An alternative is auto-gestation which would require feeding on what is excreted. Cragg has pondered the details in Hieronymus Bosch's work and it pleases him that *On the Savannah* with the gigantic syphon and extended bottles has a heritage. He envisages these double-ended forms with biomorphic middles standing across a room, formidable and emotionally stiring. The bottles become a buffalo and the mortar and pestle a long-necked swan. One can hope, too, as an artist, to be prophetic. Bosch's creatures in the left panel of *The Temptation of St Anthony* foretell the spaceships we imagine reaching Mars and ET's friends. We look at a Bosch or any pre-photographic work of art and depend on it for facts. Some are outdated, the people were dressed in leather jerkins and curing disease by blood-letting. On the other hand their sadism and libido is not unrecognisable. We still need art which releases nightmarish visions. It combats the passions that foster mob violence, born of timidity, and re-directs them to a twilight zone where the imagination counts. A beautiful example of a frightening theme is the sculpture entitled *Vivarium*. One tree divided

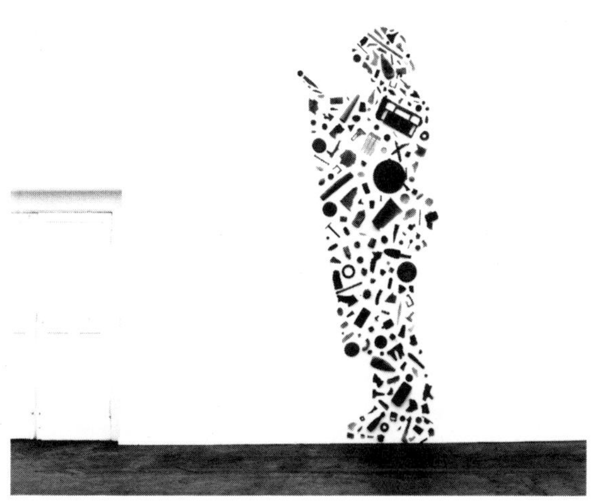

Policeman 1981 (Lisson Gallery, London).

mid-way, like 'Bermuda shorts', Cragg says, another is from roughbarked pine and the third shaped like an ice-hockey stick. The clinging tyres suggest the perversion it is to manufacture substances that do not rot once they become redundant. In luminous marble plaster, the sculpture is a marvellous spectre.

For some weeks in the winter of 1987–88 Cragg kept a collection of Seiff stuffed animals in his flat (amidst his children). He then took them away and in the studio, they were stiffened by paint, prior to casting, thereby acquiring histaminic eyes. Cragg imagined them higgledy-piggledy in two spiralling chains. The analogy to DNA, which fascinates Cragg, is one reason for making the work. Imitation animals are a natural way of satirising painful ideas of the pathetic weakness of human life; the least disturbing analogy being the awkward acquisition of motor control in infants and the same loss of it in old age. There is very little left unexposed in Cragg. Occasionally the imagery will seem suburban, or the large works bombastic. He has to keep going near to areas which are ugly and banal in order to advance his investigation. The division of the modern world into what is really surrounding us and what we stubbornly hold in romantic fantasy is an outworn, class-ridden and arrogant habit. In fact it takes a romantic artist, as well as a crusading and fantastical one, to feel the need to leave for the future something antidotal and restorative and magnificently conceived.

Catherine Lampert

1. 'Interview with Demosthenes Davvetas', *Tony Cragg*, Société des Expositions du Palais des Beaux-Arts de Bruxelles, 1985, p. 31.

2. 'Tony Cragg interviewed by Lynne Cooke. Wuppertal, West Germany, Dec. 1986', *Tony Cragg*, Hayward Gallery, London, Arts Council of Great Britain, 1987, p. 16.

3. The Prince of Wales, delivering the keynote address to the Re-making Cities Conference, Pittsburgh, reported in the Sunday Times, February 1988.

4. Hayward Gallery, 1987, p. 64.

5. Caroline Tisdall, *Joseph Beuys*, New York, 1979, p. 269 and p. 280, quoting Beuys'.

'Energy plan for Western Man' manifesto, 1979.

6. Richard S. Westfall, *Never at Rest. A Biography of Issac Newton*, Cambridge, 1980.

7. Ibid.

8. Mary Shelly, *Frankenstein*, Harmondsworth, 1985, p. 97.

9. Ibid., p. 97.

10. Ibid., p. 100.

11. Hayward Gallery, 1987, p. 14.

CATALOGUE

We thank the following
for lending sculpture from their collections:

Buchmann Gallery, Basel
Crousel-Robelin Gallery, Paris
Konrad Fischer Gallery, Düsseldorf
Ida Gianelli, Genoa
Marian Goodman Gallery, New York
Bernd Klüser Gallery, Munich
Lisson Gallery, London
Lisa and Tucci Russo, Turin
Saatchi Collection, London
Union Bank of Switzerland, Wil
Werkstatt Kollerschlag, Kollerschlag
Private Collections

Boat 1980
150 x 400 cm, Wood
Collection Ida Gianelli, Genoa

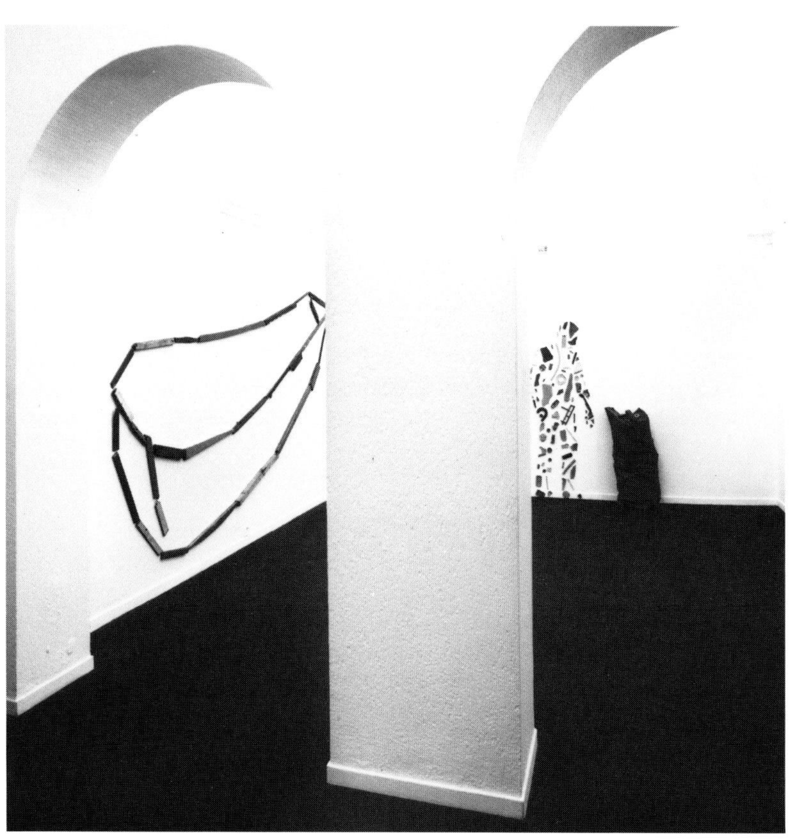

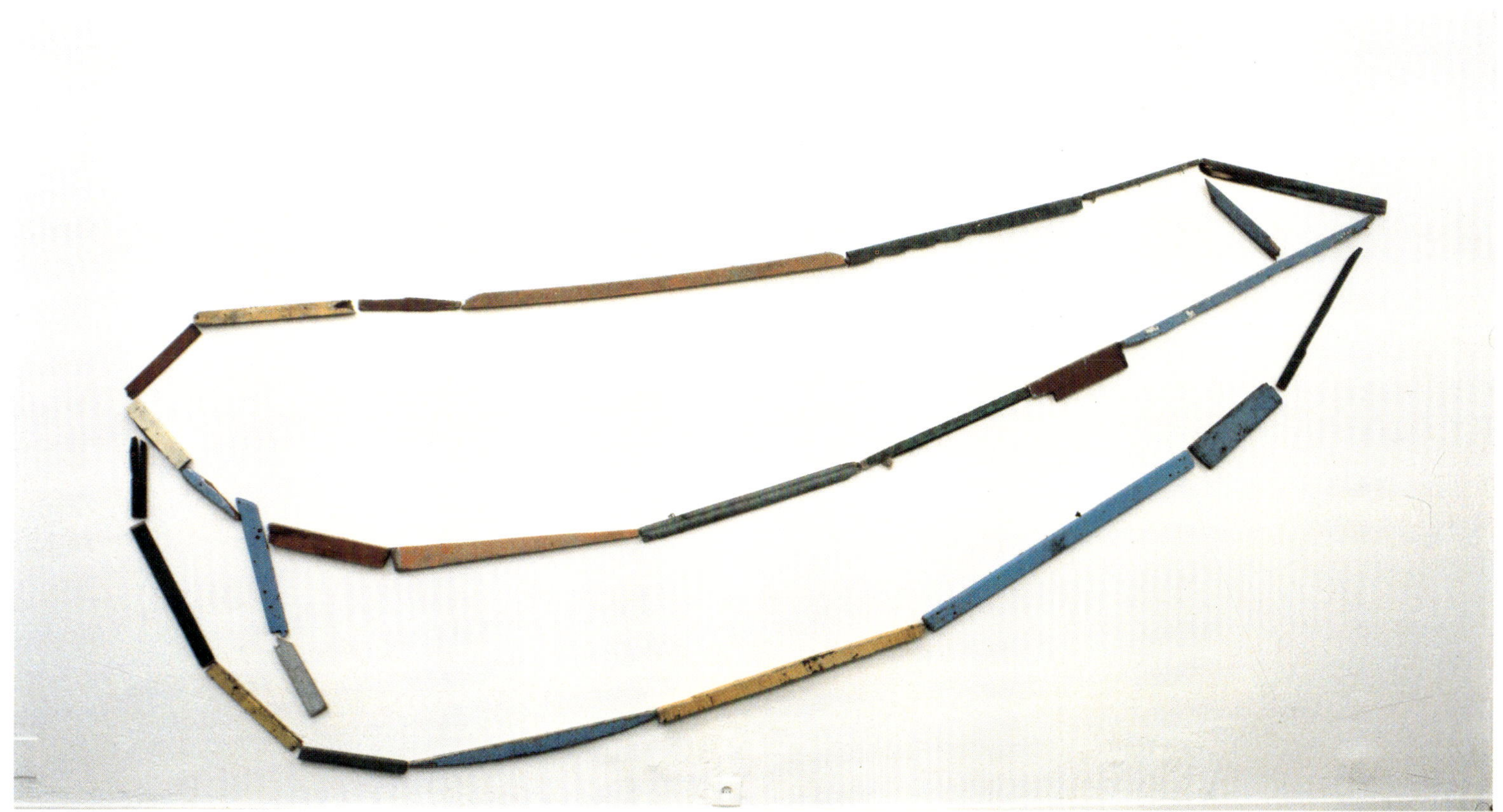

Policeman 1988
400 x 120 cm, Blue plastic
Courtesy Bernd Klüser Gallery,
Munich

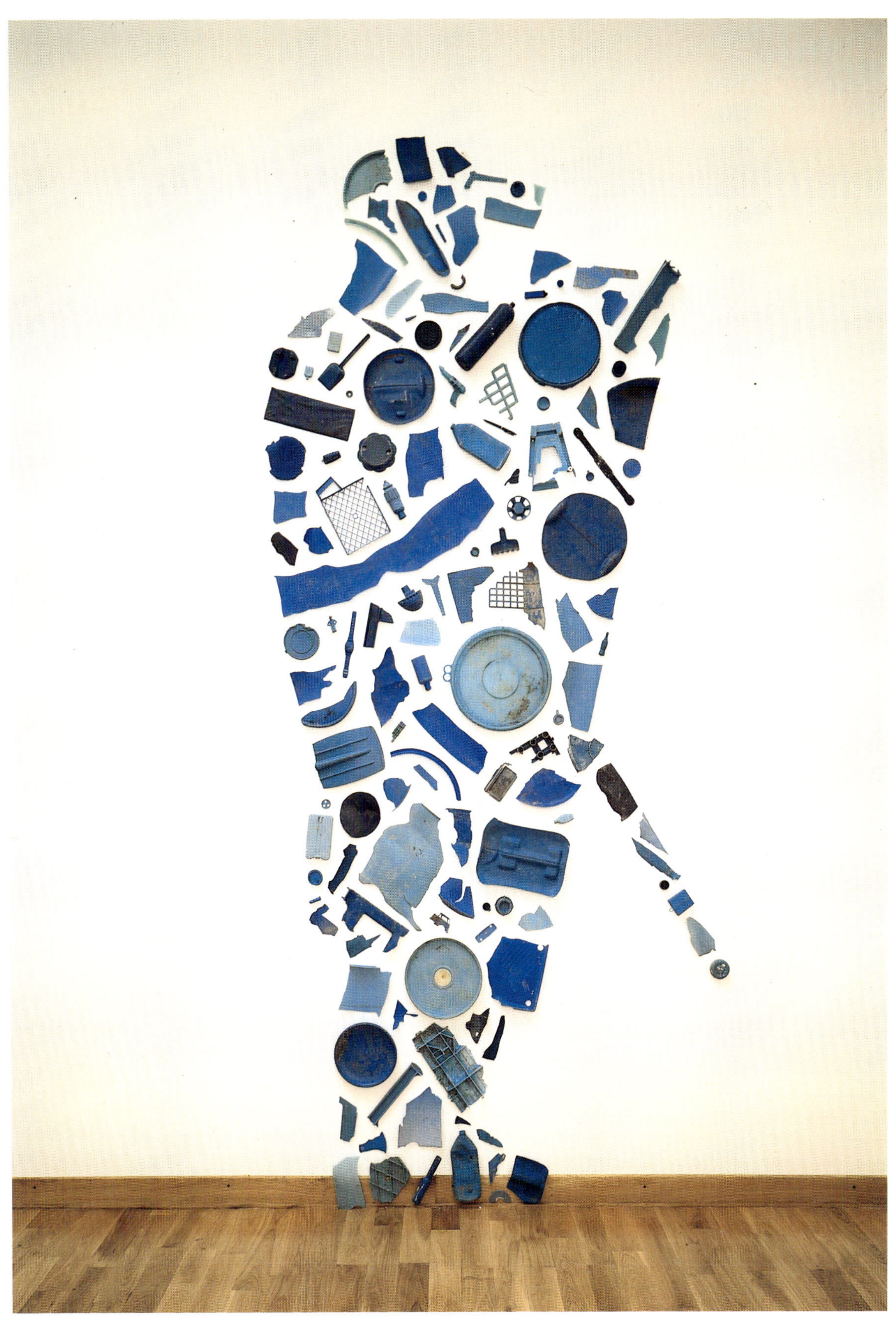

Guglie 1987
245 x 53, 190 x 46, 212 x 62 cm
Wood, rubber, concrete
Courtesy Tucci Russo Gallery,
Turin

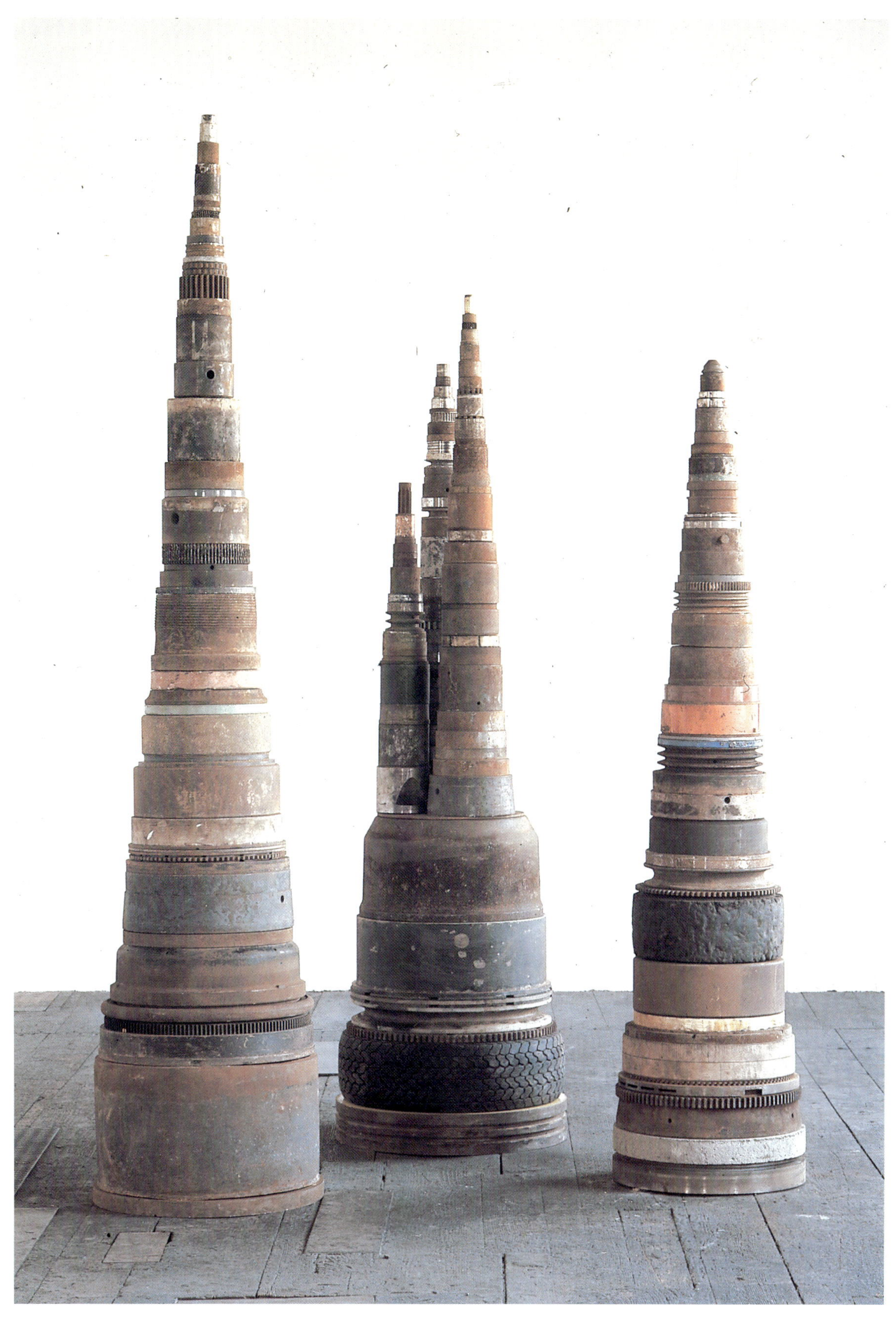

Inverted Sugar Crop 1987
100 x 200 x 100 cm, Bronze, steel
Saatchi Collection, London

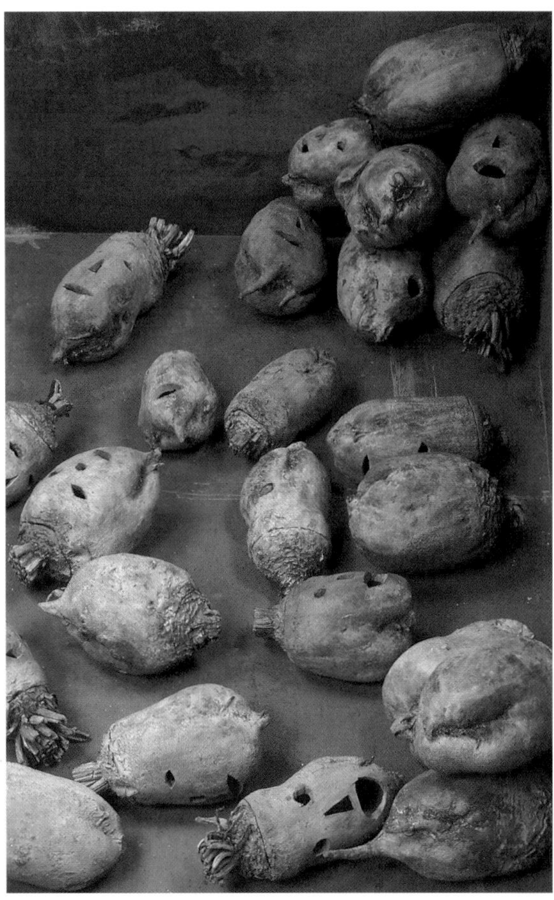

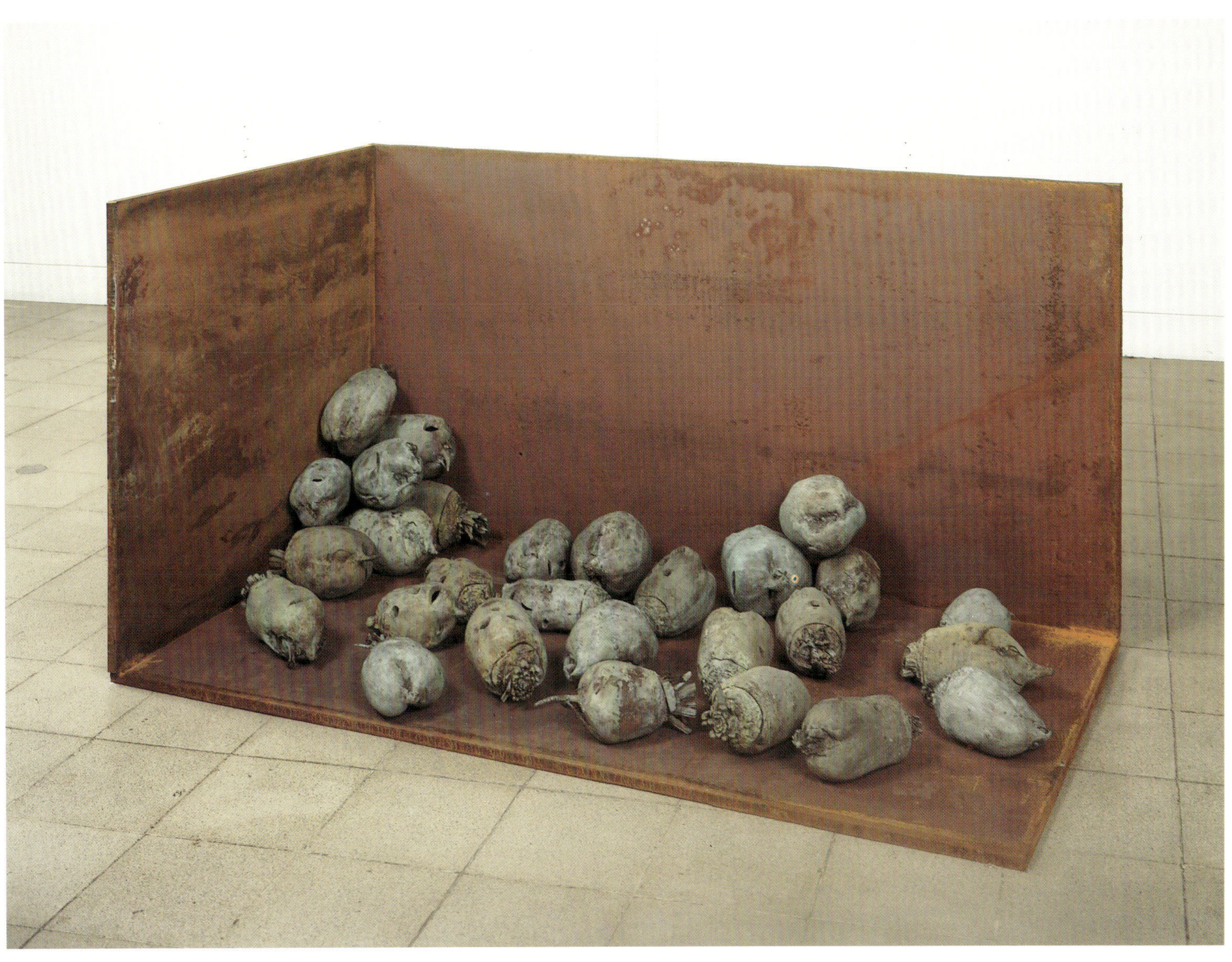

Pangea 1987
35 x 350 x 200 cm, Steel
Courtesy Werkstatt Kollerschlag,
Kollerschlag

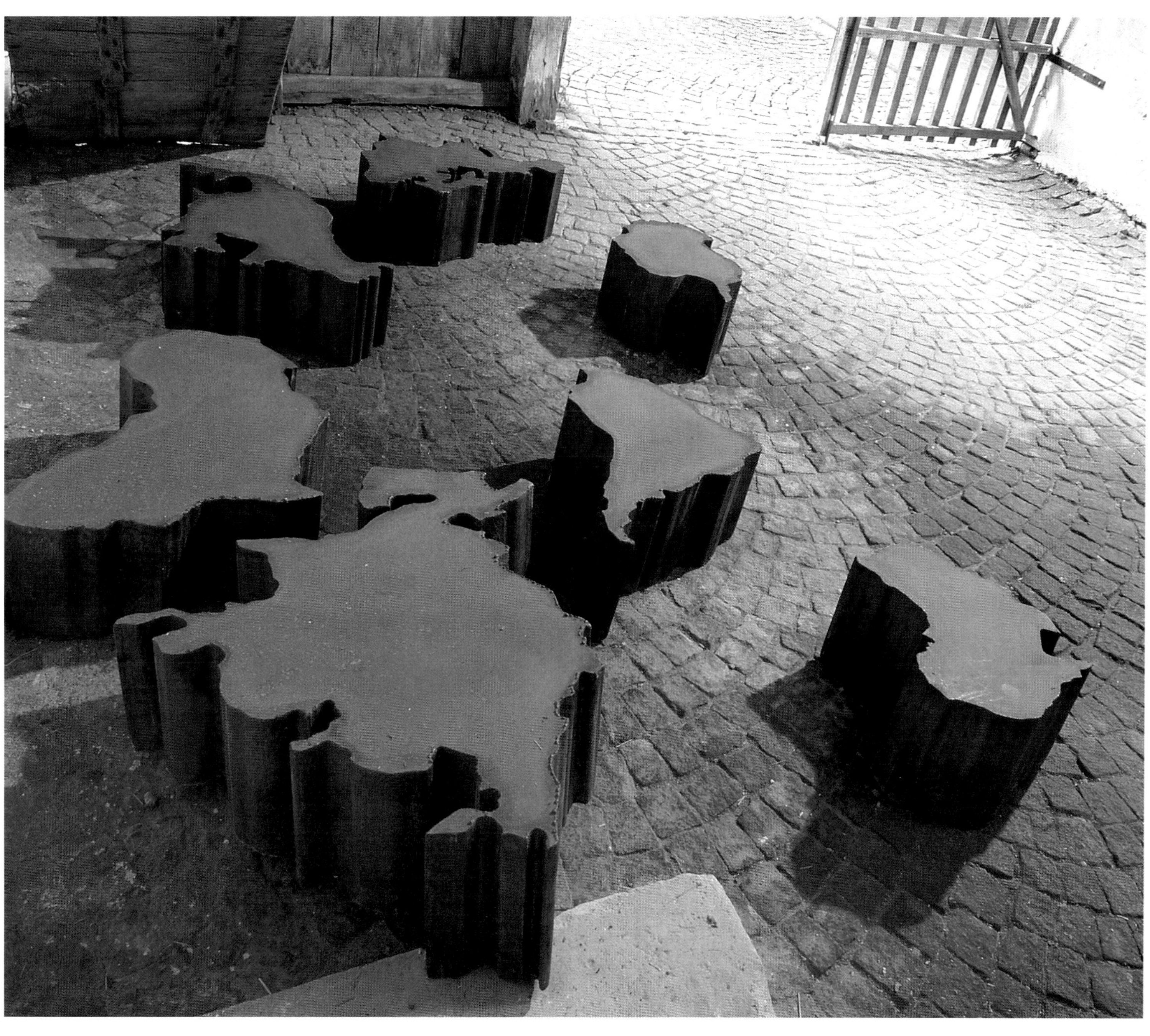

Bestückung 1987/88
210 x 200 x 80 cm, Steel
Courtesy Buchmann Gallery,
Basel

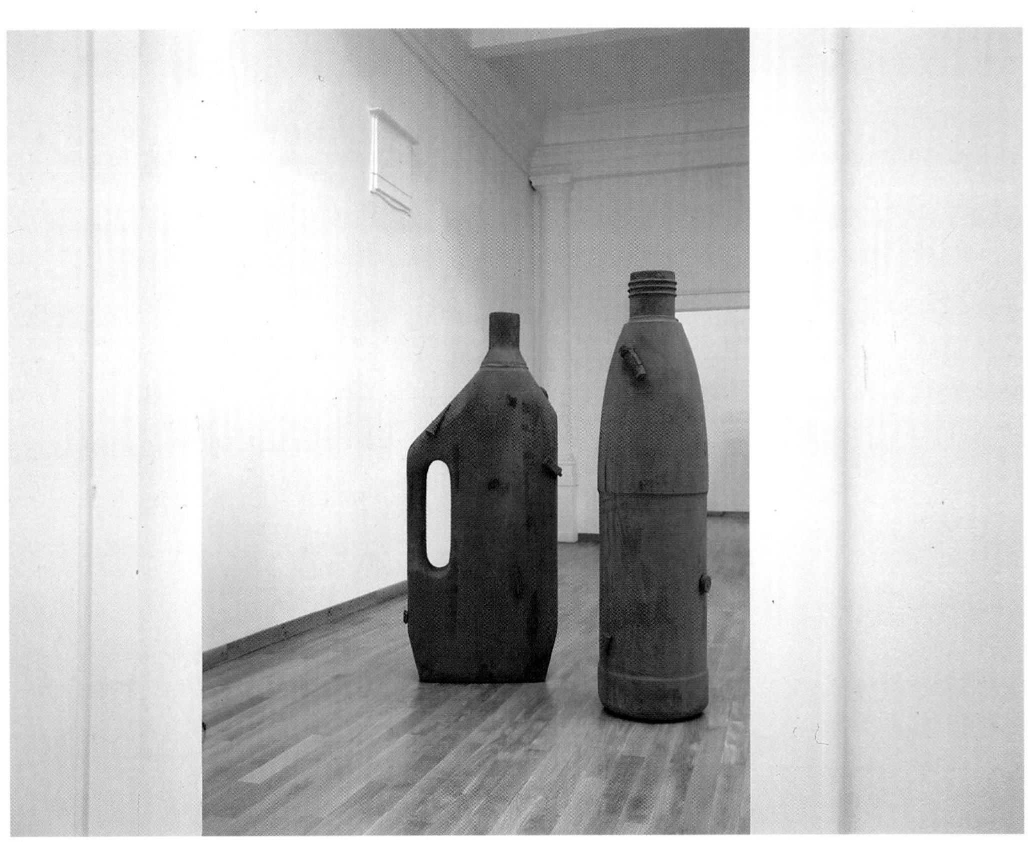

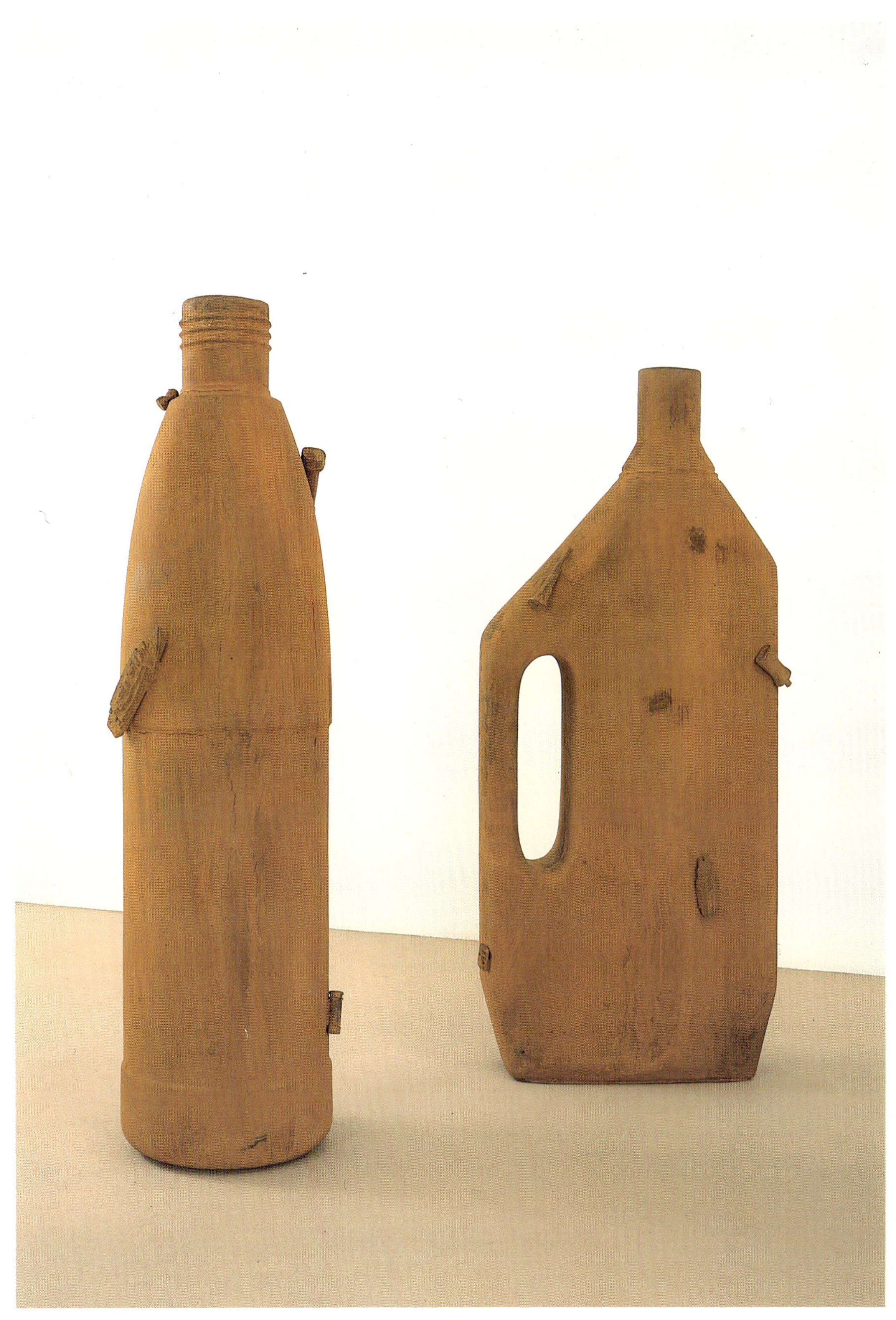

Mother's Milk II 1988
90 x 192 x 142 cm, Bronze
Courtesy Lisson Gallery,
London

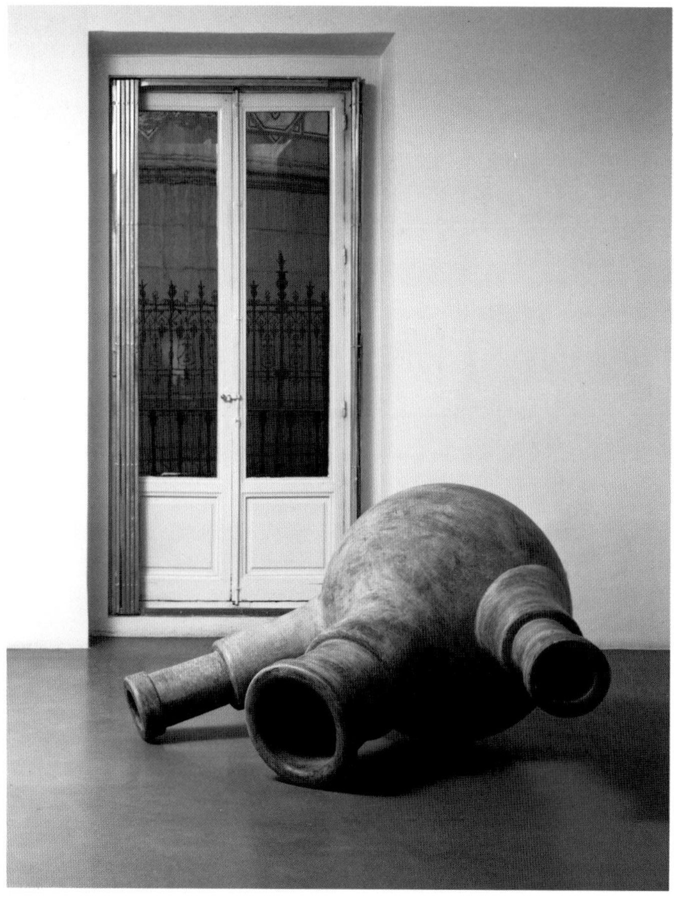

Mother's Milk I 1987
Installation
Marga Paz Gallery,
Madrid

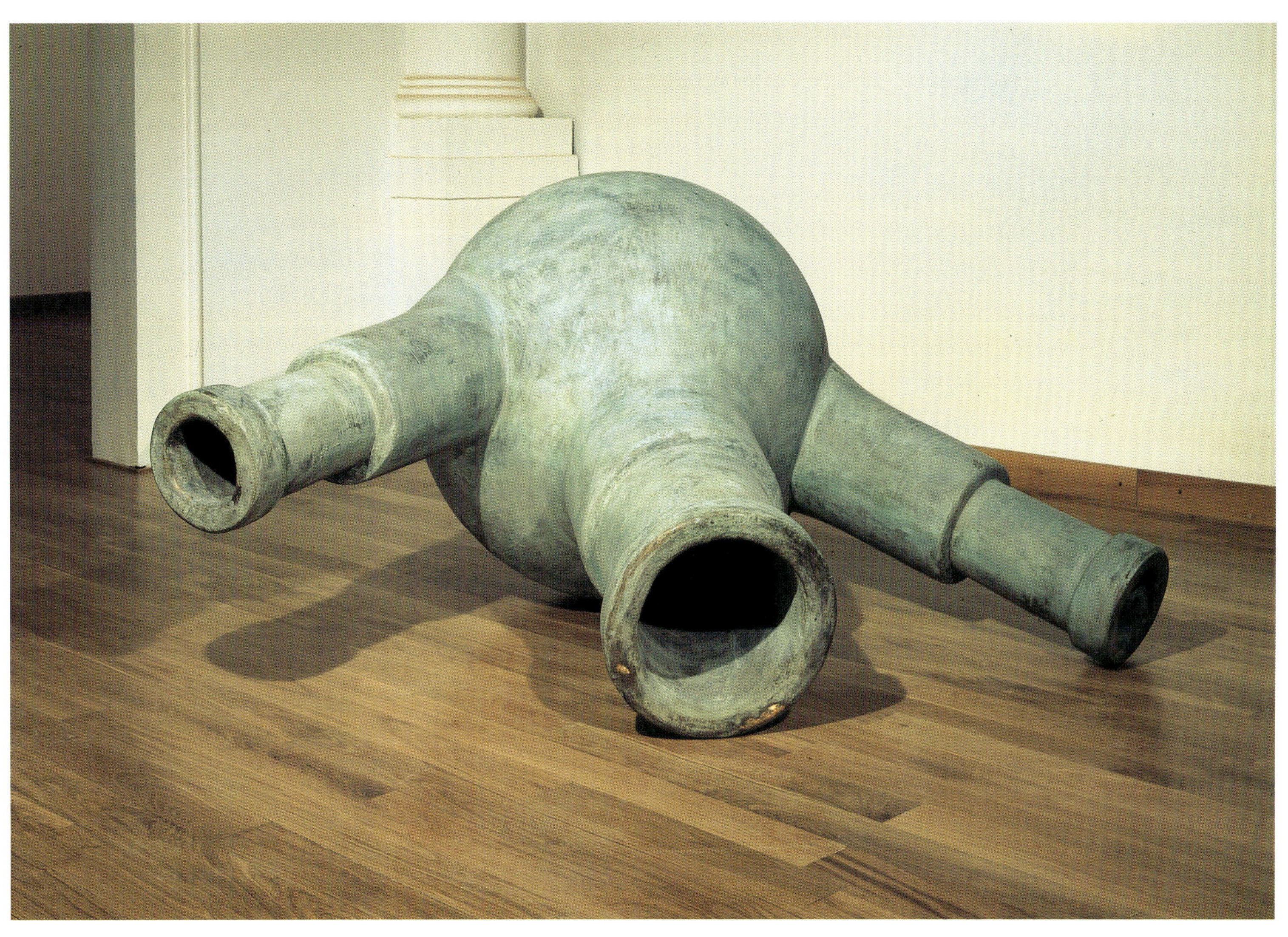

Silicate 1988
75 x 300 x 190 cm, Glass, wood

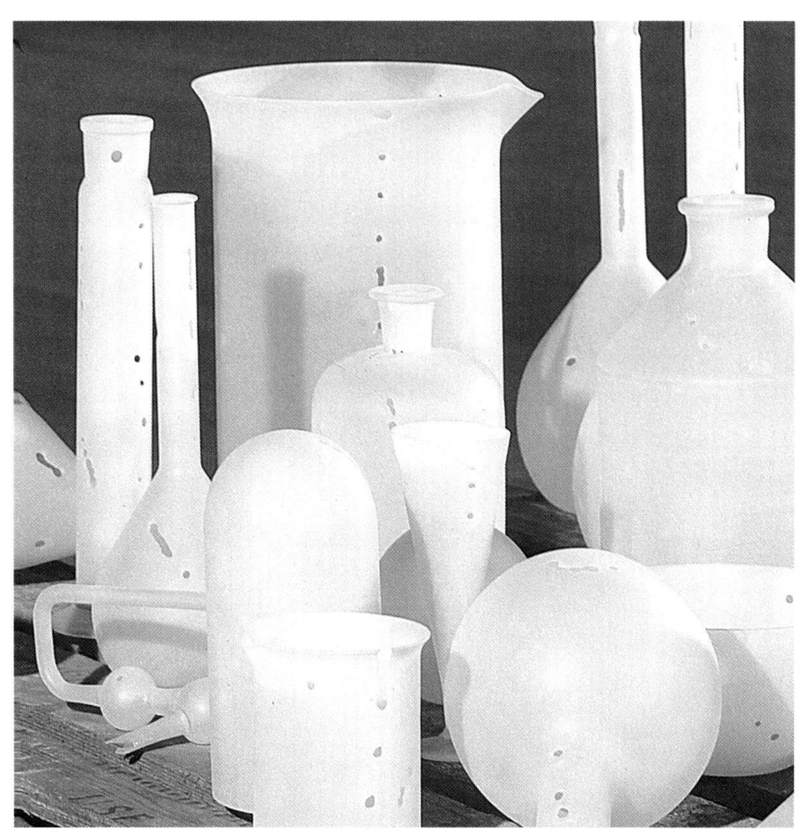

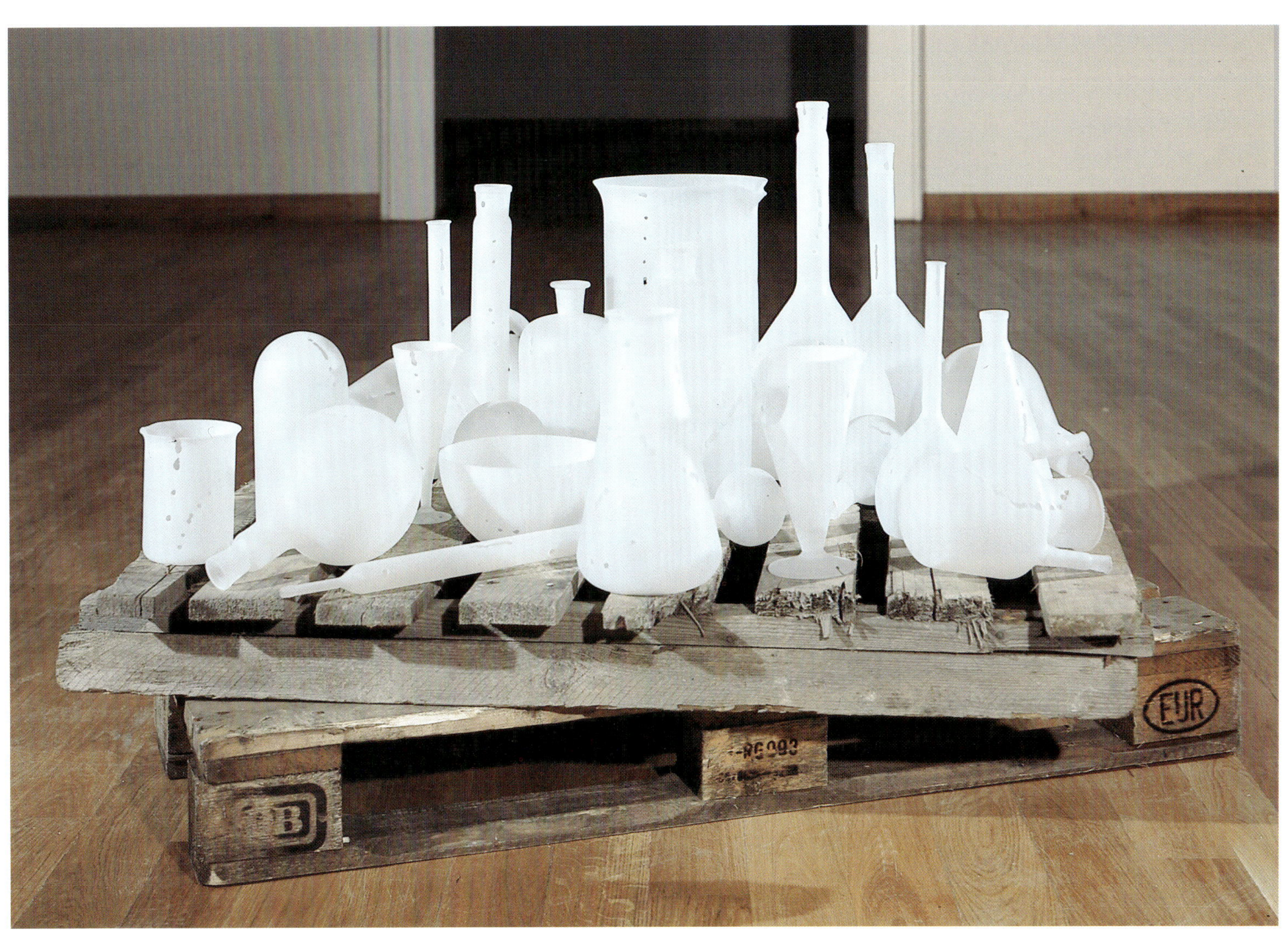

Generations 1988
70 x 200 x 250 cm,
Plaster of Paris
Courtesy Konrad Fischer Gallery,
Düsseldorf

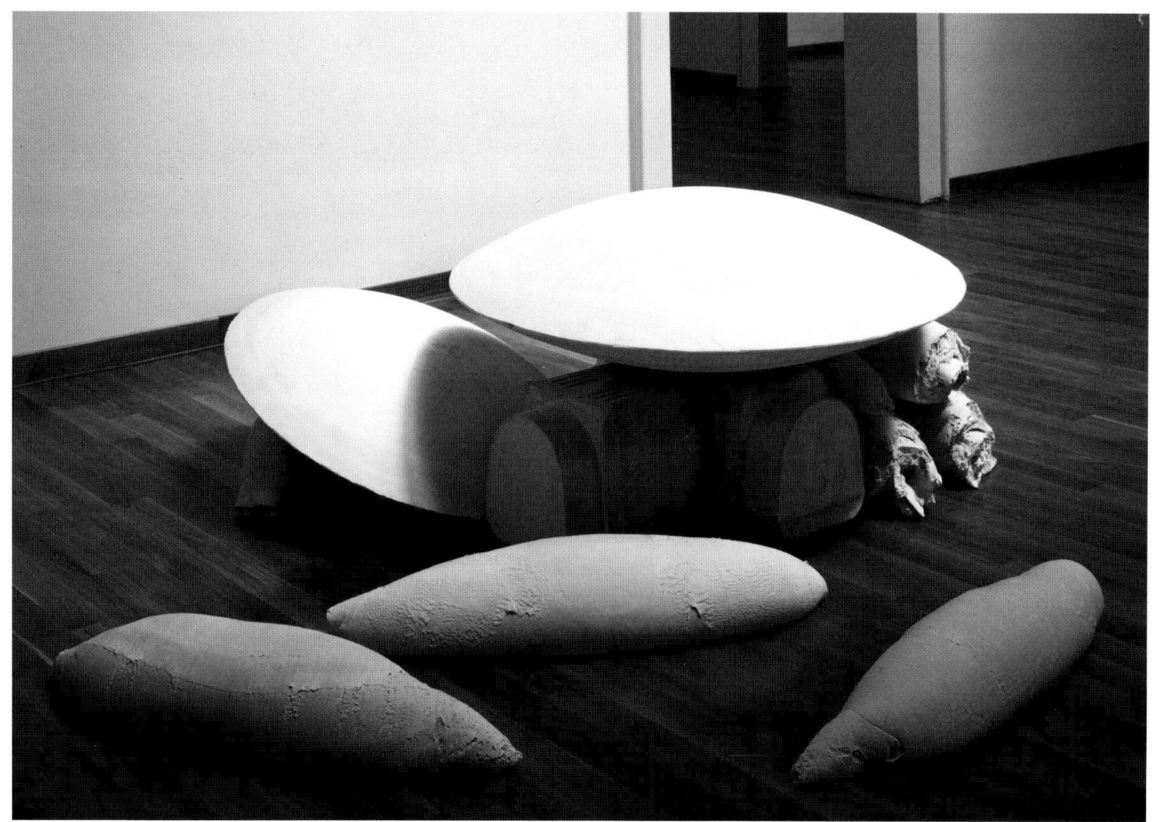

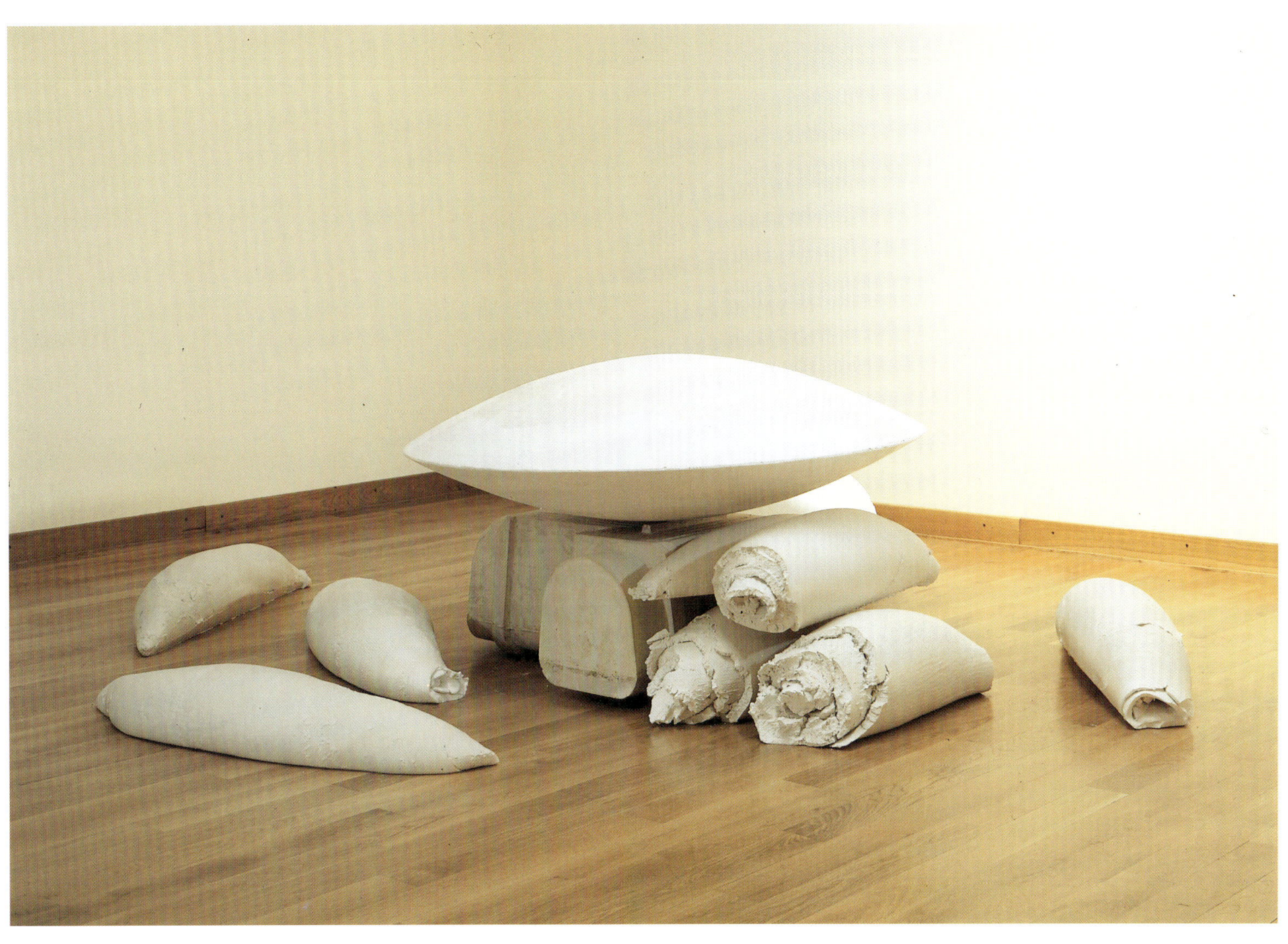

Vivarium 1988
110 x 140 x 108 cm,
Plaster of Paris

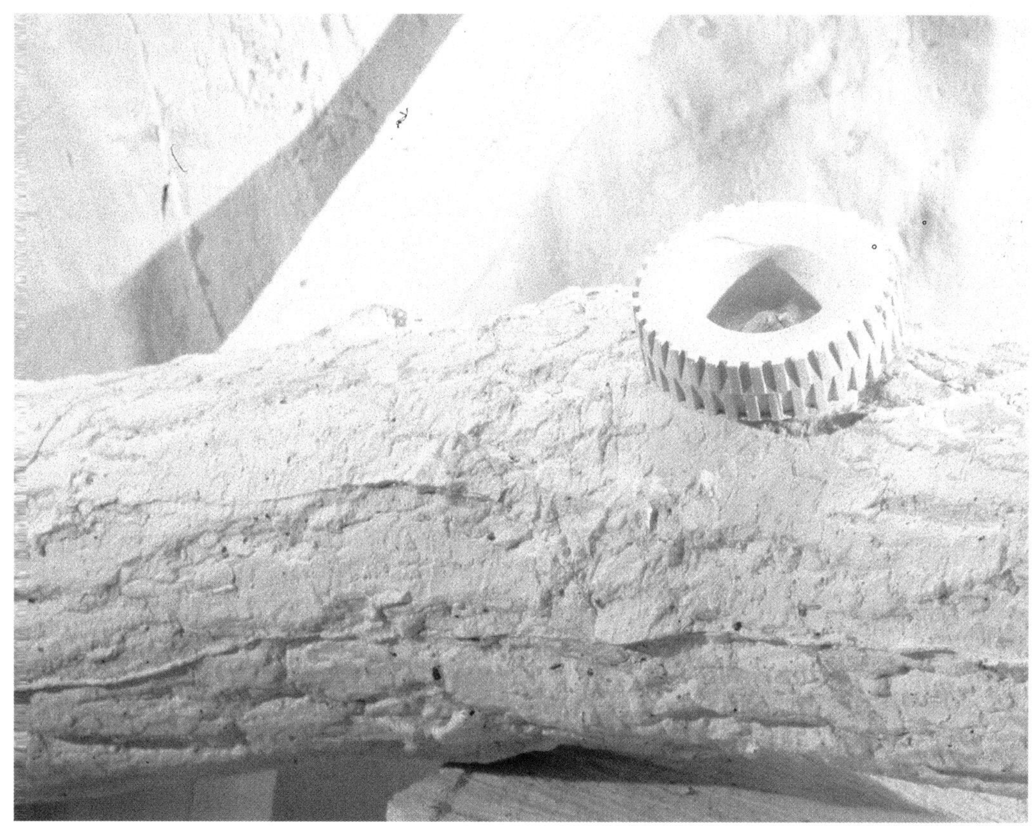

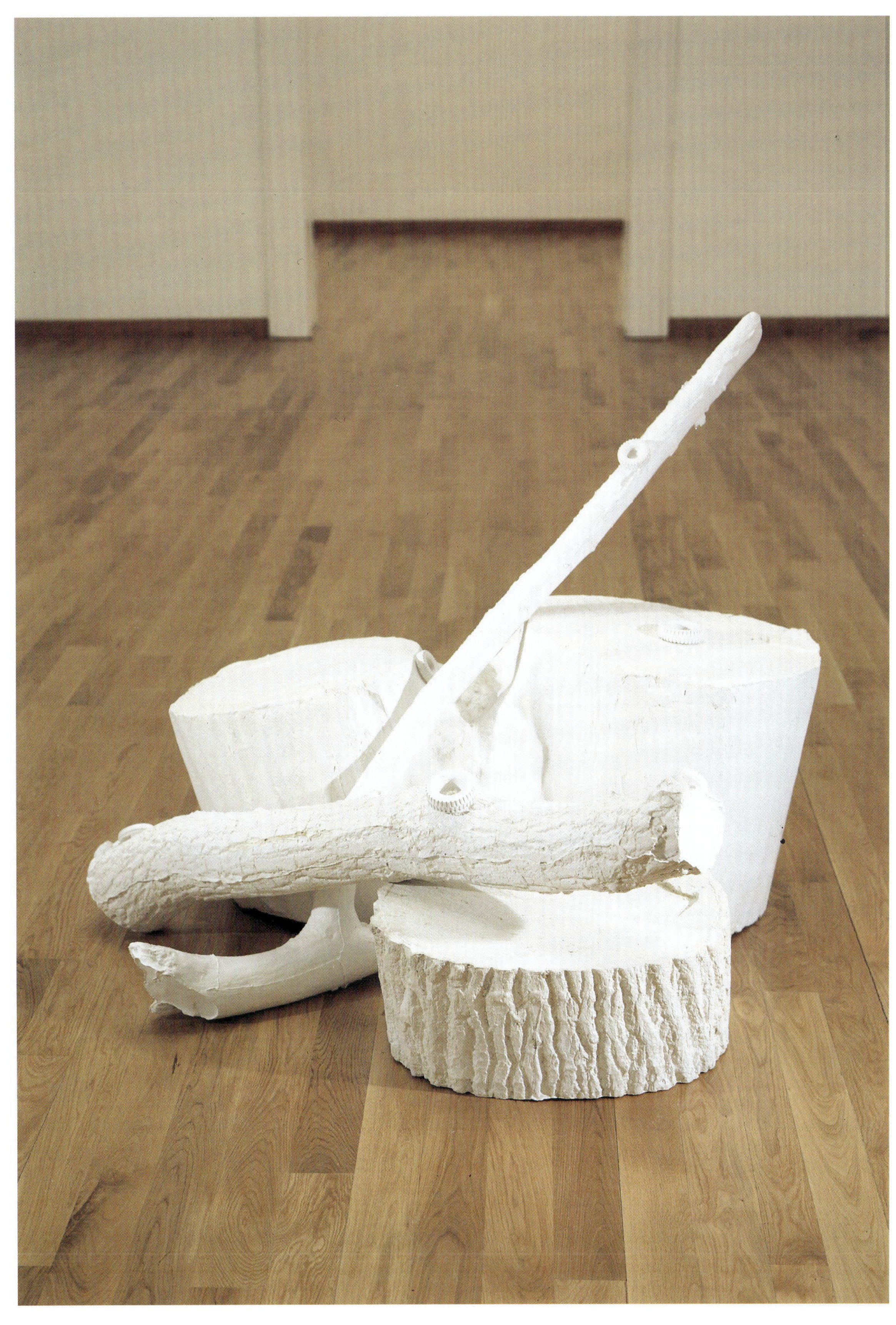

Loco 1988
160 x 240 x 220 cm, Wood
Courtesy Marian Goodman Gallery,
New York

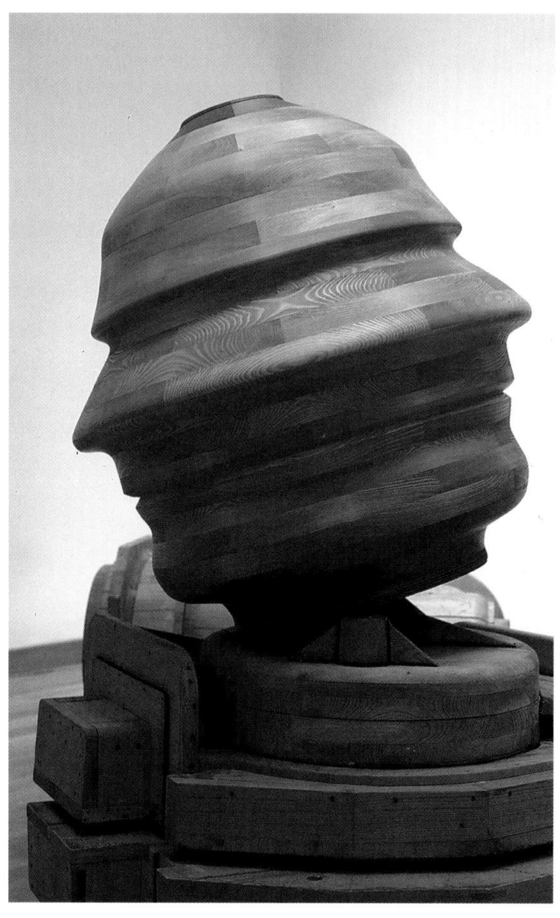

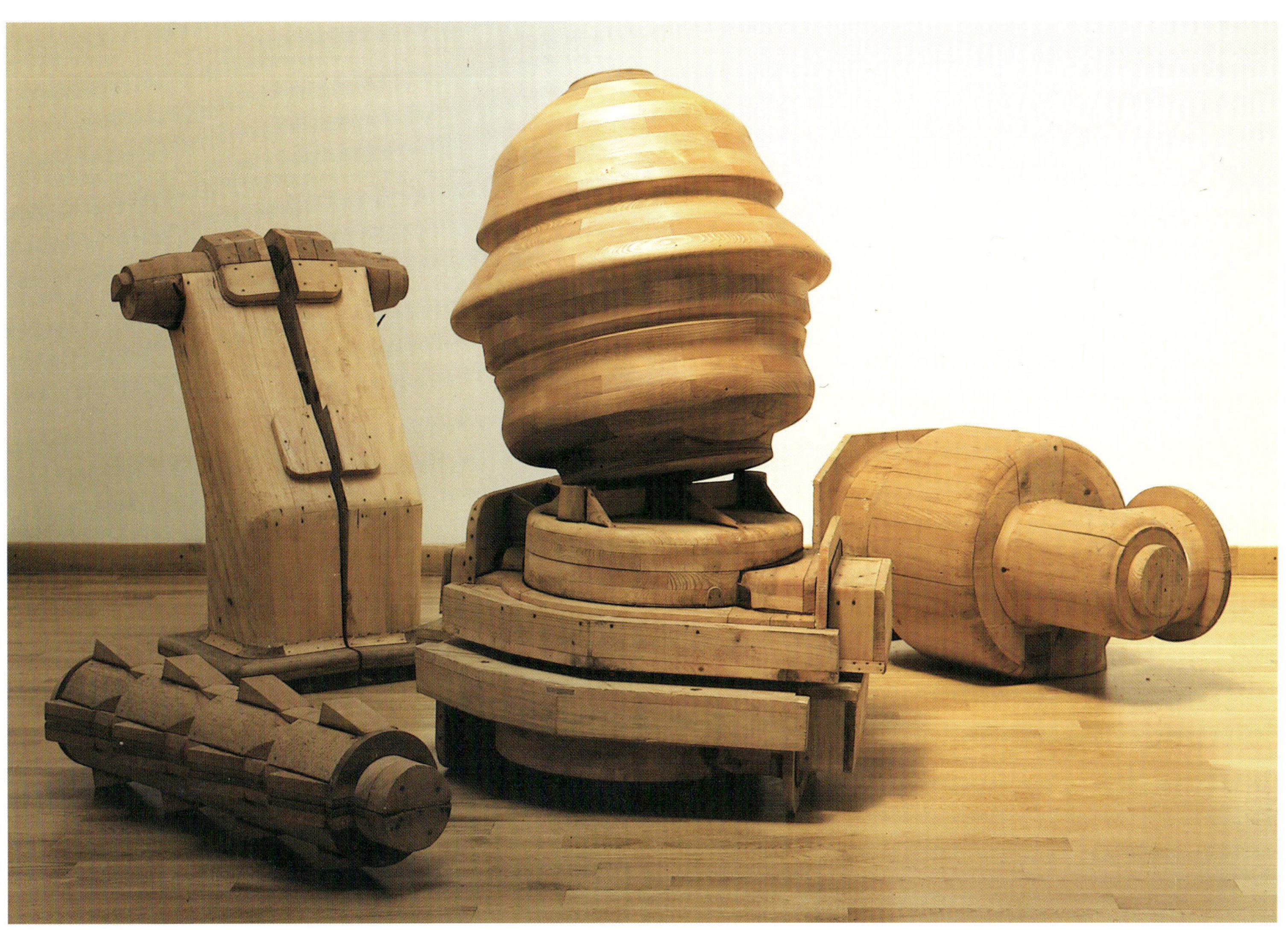

Bench 1988
186 x 250 x 90 cm, Sandstone
Collection
Union Bank of Switzerland,
Wil

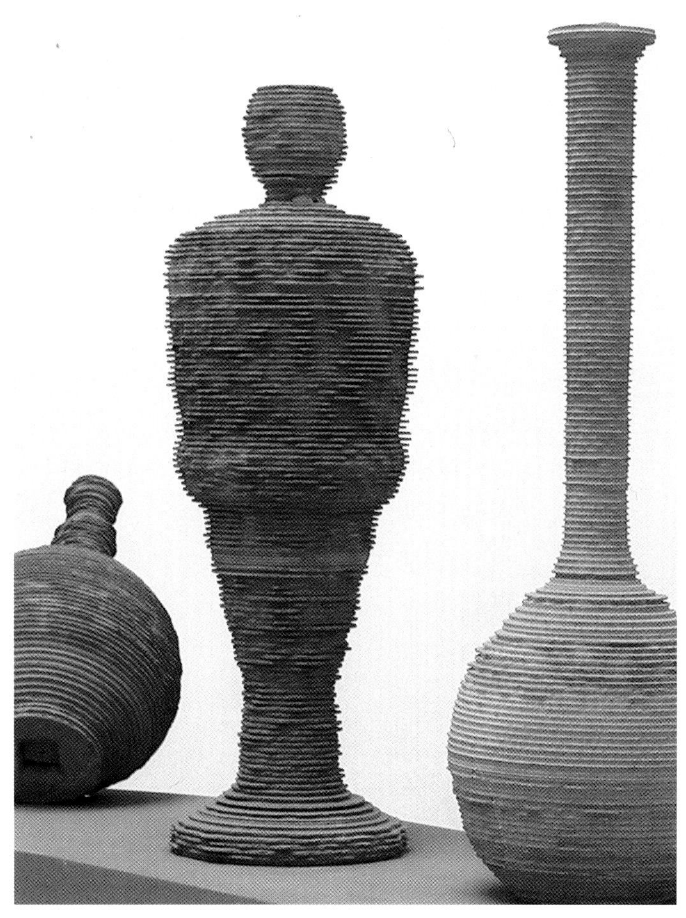

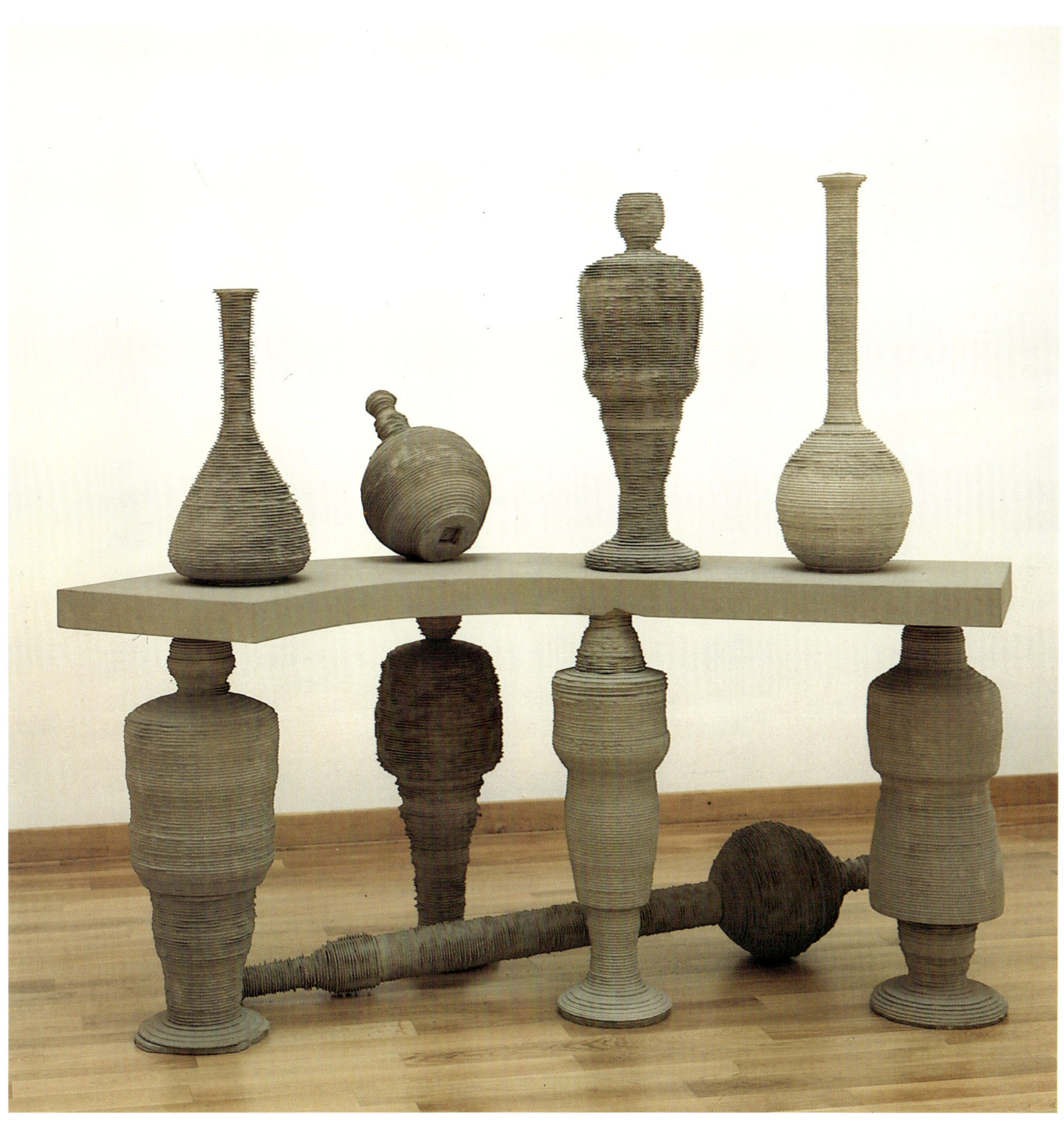

Code Noah 1988
275 x 100 x 100 cm, Bronze
Courtesy
Marian Goodman Gallery,
New York

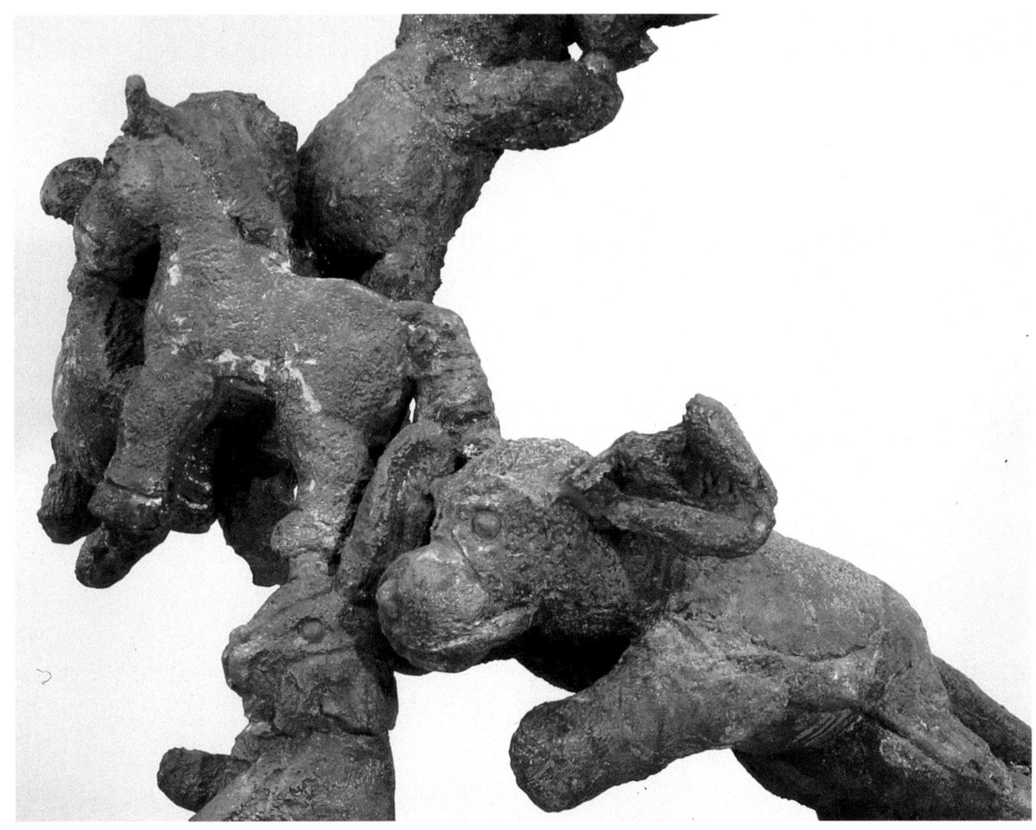

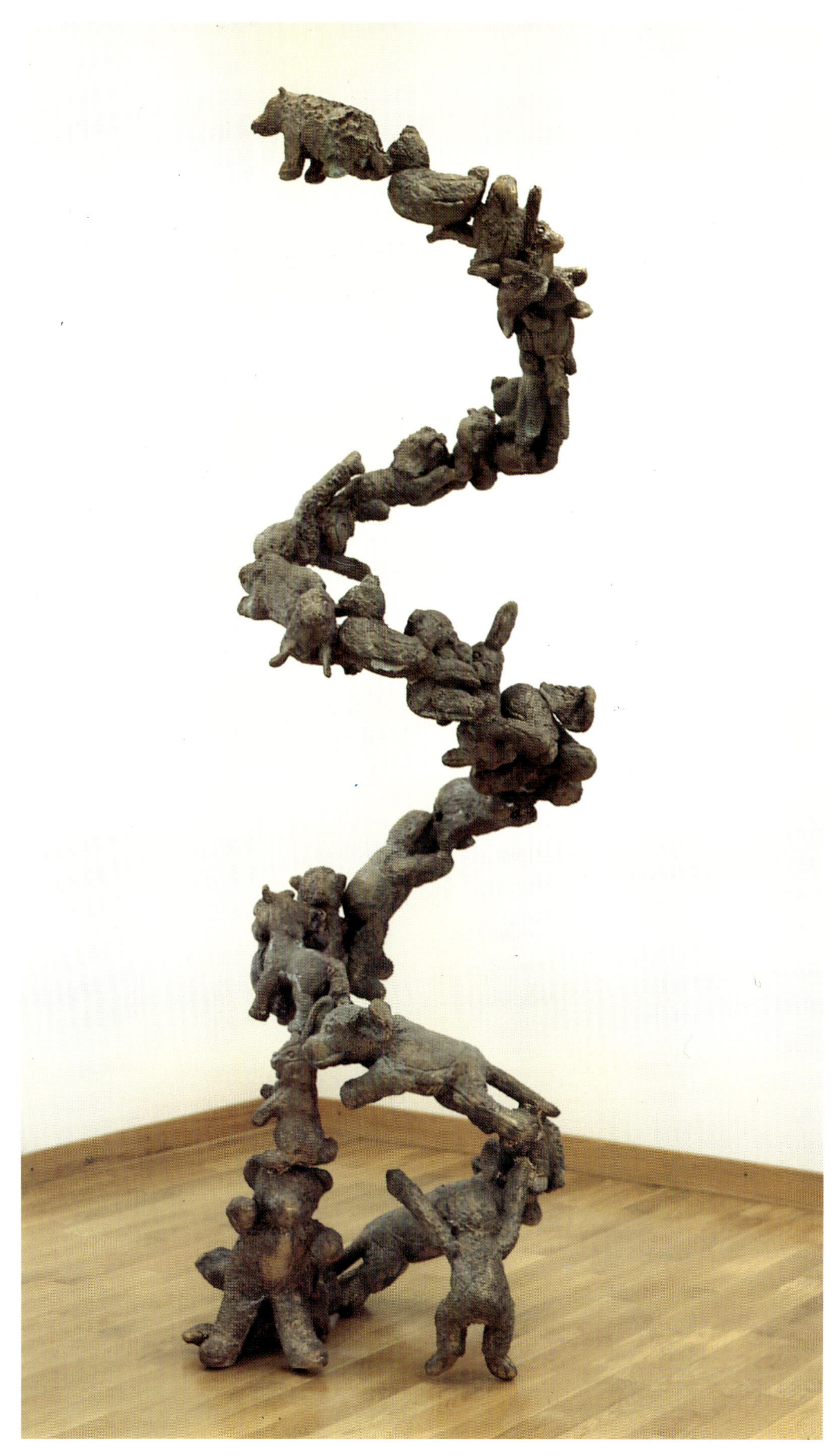

Untitled 1988
110 x 220 x 200 cm, Steel
Courtesy
Crousel-Robelin Gallery,
Paris

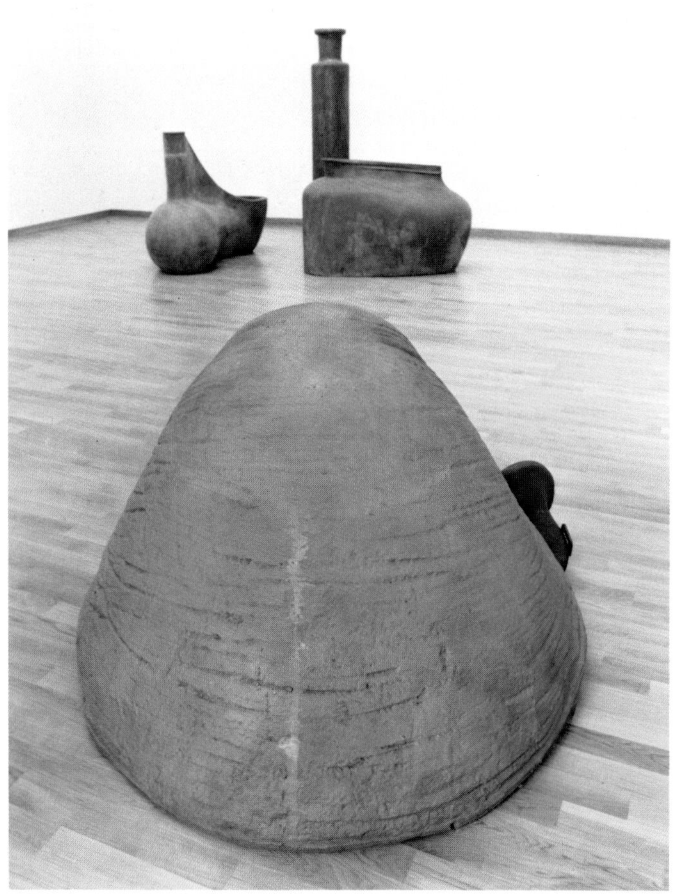

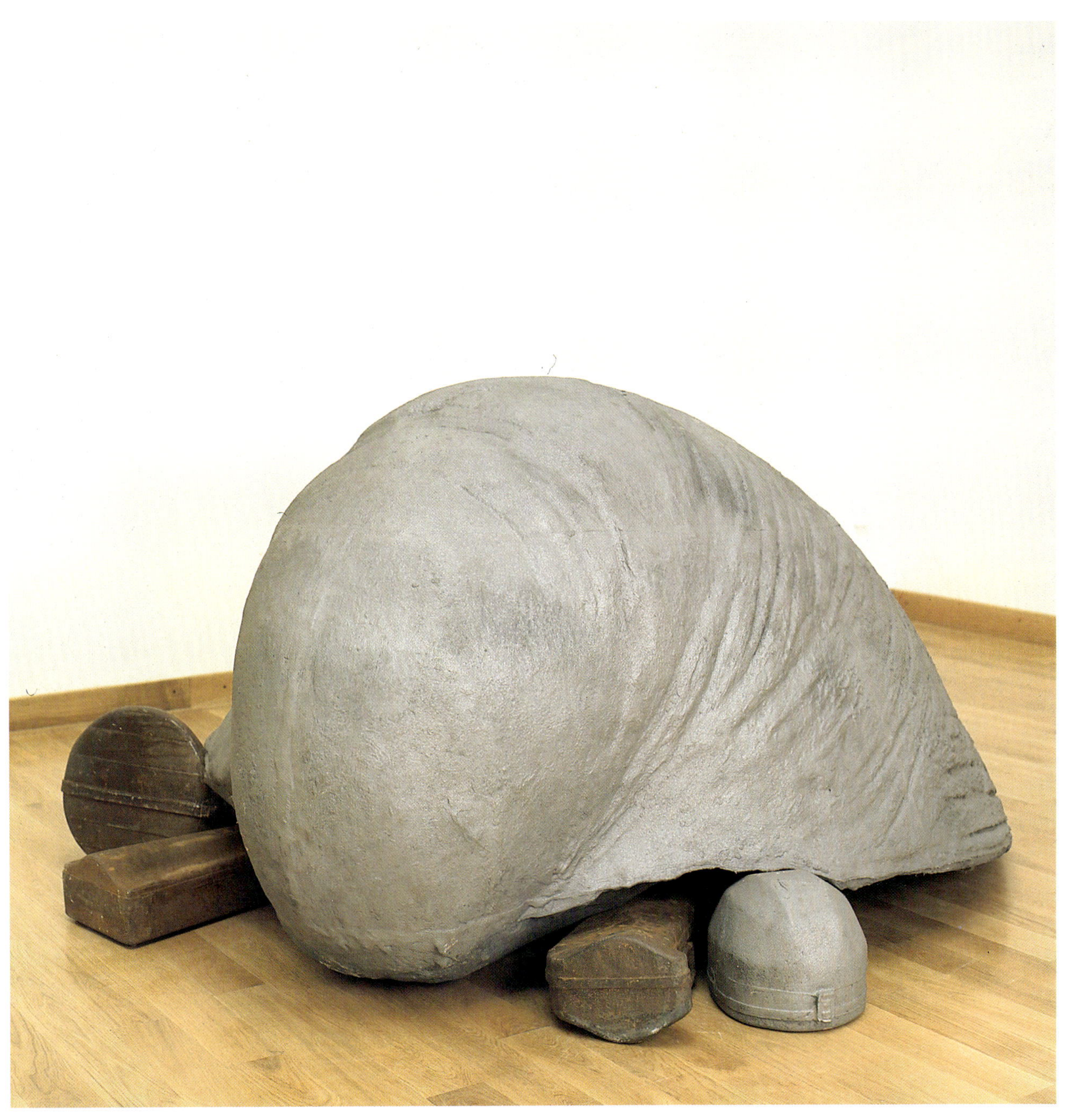

On the Savannah 1988
225 x 400 x 300 cm, Bronze
Courtesy Lisson Gallery,
London

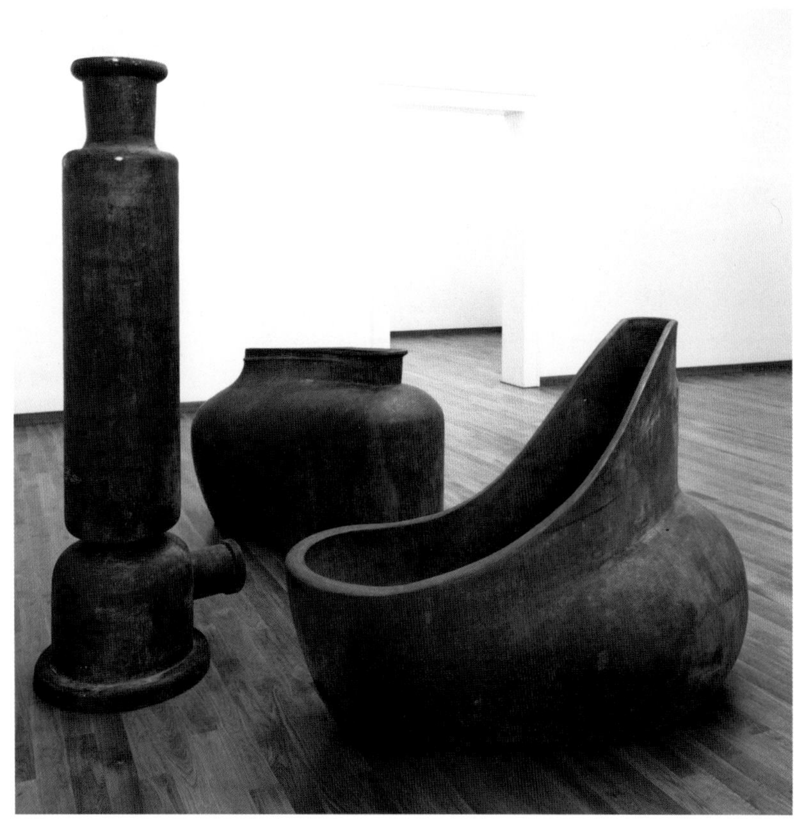

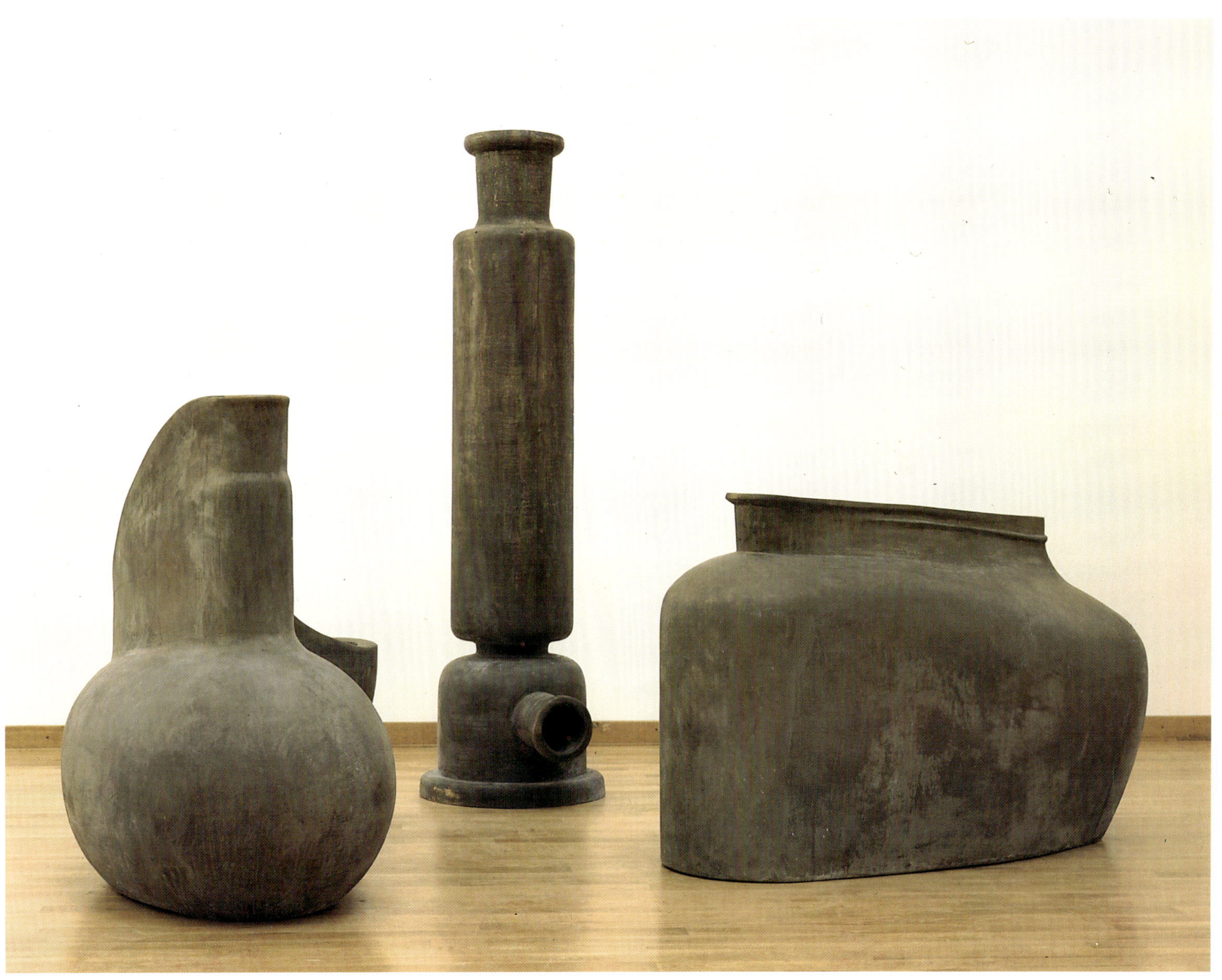

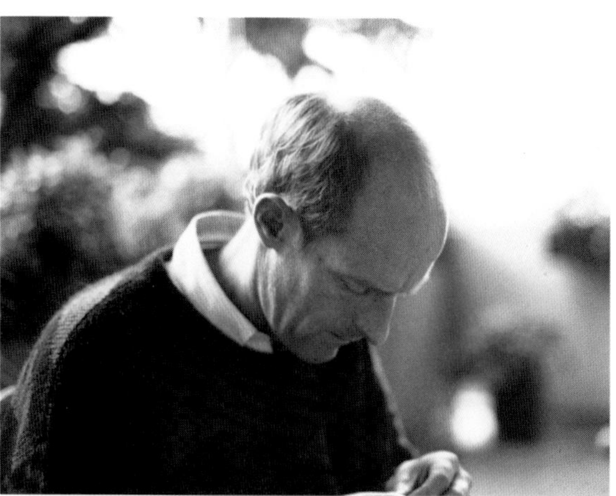

Tony Cragg 1949 born in Liverpool

Selected Solo Exhibitions

1979
Lisson Gallery, London
Lützowstrasse Situation, Berlin
Künstlerhaus Weidenallee, Hamburg

1980
Arnolfini Gallery, Bristol
Konrad Fischer, Düsseldorf
Lisson Gallery, London
Chantal Crousel, Paris
Lützowstrasse Situation, Berlin
Lucio Amelio, Naples
Franco Toselli, Milan
Saman Gallery, Genova

1981
Schellmann & Klüser, Munich
Musée d'Art et d'Industrie, St-Etienne
Whitechapel Art Gallery, London
Nouveau Musée, Lyon
Front Room, London
Von der Heydt Museum, Wuppertal
Vaccuum, Düsseldorf

1982
Badischer Kunstverein, Karlsruhe
Kanransha Gallery, Tokyo
Nisshin Gallery, Tokyo
Marian Goodman, New York
Nouveau Musée, Lyon
Chantal Crousel, Paris
Büro Berlin
Schellmann & Klüser, Munich
Lisson Gallery, London
Konrad Fischer, Düsseldorf
Rijksmuseum Kröller-Müller, Otterlo

1983
Lucio Amelio, Naples
Marian Goodman, New York
Kunsthalle, Berne
Art & Project, Amsterdam
Thomas Cohn, Rio de Janiero
Galerie Buchmann, St Gallen
Toselli Gallery, Milan

1984
Yarlow & Salzmann, Toronto
De Vleeshal, Middelburg, Holland
Louisianna Museum of Modern Art, Humlebaek,
  Denmark
Schellmann & Klüser, Munich
Marian Goodman, New York

Kanransha Gallery, Tokyo
Crousel-Hussenot, Paris
Kölnischer Kunstverein, Cologne
Tucci Russo, Turin

1985
Kunsthalle Waaghaus, Winterthur
Staatsgalerie Moderner Kunst, Munich
Donald Young Gallery, Chicago
Lisson Gallery, London
Art & Project, Amsterdam
Palais des Beaux-Arts, Brussels
ARC, Musée d'Art Moderne de la Ville de Paris
Galerie Bernd Klüser, Munich
Kestner Gesellschaft, Hannover

1986
Galerie Buchmann, Basle
Joost Declercq, Ghent
Brooklyn Museum, New York
Marian Goodman, New York
Berkeley Museum, San Francisco
Geward, Gent, Belgium
La Jolla Museum of Contemporary Art, Los Angeles
Pierre Huber, Geneva
Konrad Fischer, Düsseldorf

1987
Hayward Gallery, London
Corner House, Manchester
Tucci Russo, Turin
Kanransha, Tokyo
Marian Goodman, New York

1988
Galerie Marga Paz, Munich
Galerie Buchmann, Basle
Galerie Crousel-Robelin, Paris
Foksal Gallery, Warsaw
Silo, Val de Valse

Selected Group Exhibitions

1975
Brunel University, Uxbridge
RCA Gulbenkian Hall, London

1976
Ecole des Beaux-Arts, Metz

1977
Lisson Gallery, London
Fine Arts Building, New York
RCA Degree Show, London
Silver Jubilee Sculpture Show, Battersea Park, London

1978
JA − NA − PA III, Paris

1979
Lisson Gallery, London
Europa − Kunst der 80er Jahre, Stuttgart

1980
B Meadows at the Royal College of Art, Cambridge
Nouva Immagine, Triennale, Milan
A Perspective, Basel
Aperto '80, Venice Biennale
Kunst in Europa na '68', Museum für Hedendaagse Kunst,
Ghent

1981
Enciclopedia, Museum of Contemporary Art, Modena
Through the Summer, Lisson Gallery, London
The Motor Show, Front Room, London
British Sculpture in the Twentieth Century, Whitechapel
Gallery, London

1982
Aspects of British Art Today, Metropolitan Museum of Art,
Tokyo and tour
Indian Triennale, New Delhi
De la Catastrophe, Centre d'Art Contemporain, Geneva
Art and Architecture, ICA, London
Neue Skulptur, Nächst St Stephan, Vienna
Documenta 7, Kassel
Englische Plastik Heute / British Sculpture Now,
Kunsthalle, Lucerne
Leçons des Choses, Kunsthalle, Berne
Kunst im öffentlichen Raum, Musée Savoisien, Chambéry
Kunst wird Material, Neue Nationalgalerie, Berlin
Objects and Figures, Fruitmarket Gallery, Edinburgh

1983
Truc et Troc, Leçons des Choses, ARC, Musée d'Art
Moderne de la Ville de Paris
A Pierre et Marie, une exposition en traveau, Paris
Terremoto, Naples
Sculpture 1983, Kunststichting, Rotterdam
Boltanski, Cragg, Cucchi, Disler, McLean, Sherman,
Crousel-Hussenot, Paris
The Sculpture Show, Hayward and Serpentine Galleries,
London
Transformations − New Sculpture from Britain,
XVII Bienal de Sao Paulo and tour
Arcaico Contemporaneo, (with Bill Woodrow and Mario
Merz) Museo del Sannio, Benevento
Ars '83, Kunstmuseet Ateneum, Helsinki
Summer Show, Kanransha Gallery, Tokyo
Figures and Objects, John Hansard Gallery, Southampton
La Trottola di Sirio, Centro d'Arte Contemporaneo,
Syracuse
New Art, Tate Gallery, London

1984
Sol-Mur, Musée des Beaux-Arts, Rouen
Plastiques et Plasticiens, Ziem, Martigues
Tilt l'Art à L'Œuvre, Nantes
Sydney Biennale, Art gallery of New South Wales
An International Survey of Recent Painting and Sculpture,
Museum of Modern Art, New York
Histoire de sculpture, Château des Ducs d'Eperon,
Cadillac and tour
Skulptur im 20. Jahrhundert, Merian Park, Basel
Anzinger, Cragg, Lavier, Galerie Buchmann, Basel
The British Art Show, Arts Council touring exhibition
ROSC, The Guiness Hop Store, Dublin

1985
Aureola Borealis, Oslo
Turner Prize Exhibition of Shortlisted Artists,
Tate Gallery, London
7000 Eichen, Kunsthalle Tübingen
... Möbel − Objekte und Installationen ...,
von der Heydt Museum, Wuppertal
18th Biennale, Antwerp
Alles und noch viel mehr, Kunsthalle Berne
Anniottanta, Galerie Comunale d'Arte Moderna, Bologna
The British Show, Art Gallery of Western Australia
and tour
Hayward Annual, Hayward Gallery, London

1986
Venice Biennale
Beuys zu Ehren, (Armin Zweite), Städtische Galerie
im Lenbachhaus, Munich
Entre el objeto y la imagen, Palacio de Velazquez, Madrid
and tour
Echo und Monumenten Ihrer Präzis Reise, Zurich

Englische Bildhauer, Galerie Harold Behm, Hamburg
La Sculptura, Vienna
Sonsbeek 86, Arnheim

1987
Current Affairs: British Painting and Sculpture in the 1980s,
    British Council touring exhibition in Hungary,
    Czechoslovakia and Poland
British Sculpture since 1965, Museum of Contemporary
    Art, Chicago and tour
British Art of the 1980s, Liljevalchs Konsthall, Stockholm
    and Sara Hilden Art Museum, Tampere, Finland
    (re-titled: *Britannica)*
Anderer Leute Kunst, Museum Hans Lange, Krefeld
Juxtapositions, The Institute for Art and Urban Resources,
    Long Island City, New York (with Deacon, Kapoor,
    Woodrow and others)
Documenta, Kassel
Drawing, Kanransha Gallery, Tokyo (with Buren, Fulton,
    Knoebel, McLean, Vilmouth and Palermo)
Edinburgh International, Royal Scottish Academy
    (with Deacon, Lewitt and others)

1988
Présentation & Propositions, FRAC Rhône-Alpes,
    Villa du Parc
De Verzameling, Museum van Hedendaagse Kunst,
    Antwerpen
Britannica: Vingt-Cinq Ans de Sculpture, Musée des
    Beaux-Arts André Malraux, Le Havre, Musée de
    l'Evêché, Evreux and Ecole d'Architecture de
    Normandie, Rouen; travelling to Museum van
    Hedendaagse Kunst, Antwerpen, February-March 1989

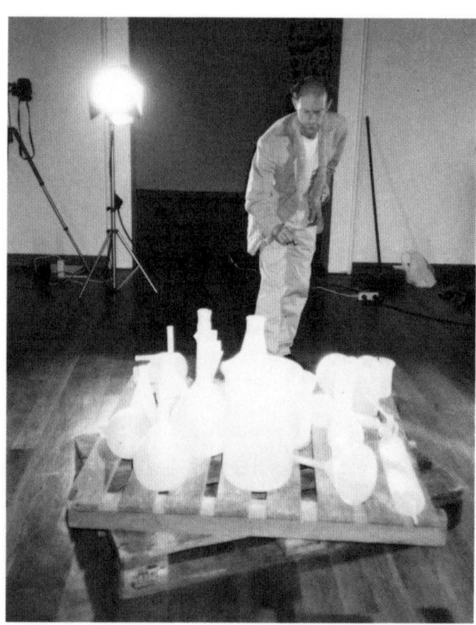

Tony Cragg
at the British Pavilion in Venice 1988

Selected Bibliography

1980
ARTICLES
Lewis Biggs: 'Tony Cragg'. *Arnolfini Review*. Bristol.
  May/June.
Edward Phelps: 'Joel Degen. Tony Cragg. Bruce McLean.
  Arnolfini Gallery. *Arts Review*. 4 July.
Stuart Morgan: 'Tony Cragg'. *Artforum*. October.
(Lisa Ponti): 'Tony Cragg'. *Domus*. November.
C. Strasser: 'Galerie Chantal Crousel, Paris'. *Flash Art*.
  November.

ESSAY
Flavio Caroli: *Nouva Immagine/New Image*.
  XVI Triennale. Milan.

1981
ARTICLES
Lynne Cooke: 'Tony Cragg at the Whitechapel'. *Artscribe*.
  March.
H. Weskott: 'Tony Cragg: Abfallskulptur des Plastik-
  zeitalters'. *Kunstforum International*. pt. 1. January.
Germano Celant: 'Tony Cragg and Industrial Platonism'.
  Artforum. November.

ESSAYS
Kunst in Europa na '68. Museum voor Hedendaagse Kunst,
  Ghent.
Bernard Ceysson: *Tony Cragg*. Musée d'Art et d'Industrie,
  Saint-Etienne.
Ursula Peters: 'Materialien und Wahrnehmung: Ein
  Zusammenspiel'. *Enciclopedia del Magico Primario in
  Europa*. Galeria Civica, Modena.
Tony Cragg. Von der Heydt Museum, Wuppertal.
Michael Newman: 'Vom Konzept zum Symbol'.
  Tony Cragg. Badischer Kunstverein, Karlsruhe.

1982
ARTICLES
R. Braxmeier: 'Badischer Kunstverein, Karlsruhe'.
  Kunstwerk. April.
Michael Newman: 'New British Sculpture'. *Art in America*.
  September.
Jean-Louis Maubant: 'Découpage/Collage à propos de
  Tony Cragg'. *Cahiers du Cric*. No. 4.
Germano Celant: 'Dall'Alfa Trainer allo Subway. *Segno*.
  September.

ESSAYS
Sandy Nairne and Nicholas Serota (eds.), Fenella Crichton:
  'Symbols, Presences and Poetry'. *Sculpture in the
  Twentieth Century*. Whitechapel Art Gallery, London.
Nobrou Nakamura: *Tony Cragg*. Kanransha Gallery,
  Tokyo.

Norbert Lynton: *Tony Cragg*. Indian Triennale,
  New Delhi, The British Council, London.
David Brown: *Aspects of British Art Today*. Metropolitan
  Art Museum, Tokyo and the British Council.
Documenta 7, Kassel.
Michael Newman: 'Tony Cragg: Fragments and Emblems'.
  Englische Plastik Heute/British Sculpure Now.
Kunstmuseum, Luzern.
Jean-Hubert Martin (interview): *Leçon des Choses*.
  Kunsthalle, Berne, Musée Savoisien, Chambéry.
Sculpture. Whitechapel Art Gallery, London (artist's
  statement reprinted from Documenta 7 catalogue).
Michael Newman: *Objects and Figures*. Fruitmarket
  Gallery, Edinburgh, Scottish Arts Council.

1983
ARTICLES
G Gintz: 'La sculpture et ses objets: l'objet de la sculpture'.
  Art Press. January.
John Roberts: 'Urban Renewal (New British Sculpture)'.
  Parachute. no. 30. Montreal. March.
Carla Stellweg: 'Tony Cragg: Marian Goodman (N.Y.)'.
  Art News. vol. 83, no. 6.
P Winter: 'Tony Cragg: Puzzlespiel und Superzeichen'.
  Kunstforum International. pt. 6. June.
P Bloch: I Presenti, 'Nouvelle sculpture: la culture de
  l'objet'. *Beaux Arts*. no. 3, June.
'Vous prenez quel apart?' (Project). *Actuel*. no. 47.
Michael Newman: 'New Sculpture in Britain'. *Art in
  America*. September.
Lynne Cooke: 'Reconsidering the new sculpture'.
  Artscribe. August.
Michael Newman: 'Figuren und Objekte: neue Skulptur in
  England'. *Kunstforum International*. June.
Carla Stellweg: 'Tony Cragg: Marian Goodman (NY)'.
  Art News. vol. 82, no. 6.

ESSAYS
Demetrio Paparoni: *Tema Celeste*. Museo Civico d'Arte
  Contemporanea di Gibellina.
Enrico Comi: *Arcaico Contemporaneo, con Tony Cragg,
  Mario Merz, Bill Woodrow*. Museo del Sannio,
  Benevento.
Paul Heftig: *Beelden/Sculpture 1983*. Rotterdam Arts
  Council.
Jean-Hubert Martin, Germano Celant: *Tony Cragg*.
  Kunsthalle, Berne.
Fenella Crichton, Kate Blacker, Paul de Monchaux: *The
  Sculpture Show: Fifty Sculptors at the Serpentine and at
  the South Bank*. Arts Council of Great Britain.

Nicholas Serota (introduction), John Roberts: 'Entangled in Imagery'. *Transformations: New Sculpture from Britain*. XVII Biennale, Sao Paulo, British Council exhibition.
Armin Wildermuth: 'Tony Cragg, Zwei Landschaften'. *Tony Cragg*. Buchmann Gallery, St Gallen and de Vleeshal.

1984
ARTICLES
Michael Newman: 'Discourse and Desire: Recent British Sculpture'. *Flash Art International*. January, and *Flash Art France*. Winter edition.
William Feaver: 'The New British Sculpture'. *Art News*. vol. 83, no. 1.
Nicholas Serota: 'Transformations – New Sculpture from Britain (40)'. *Artefactum*. February-March.
Christian Besson: 'Tony Cragg'. *Public* no. 1.
Nena Dimitriejevic: 'Sculpture after Evolution'. *Flash Art*. April-May.
Kenneth Baker: 'Marian Goodman Gallery, New York'. *Art in America*. September.
Andrew Brighton: review of British Art Show. *Art Monthly*. December/January 1984-85.

ESSAYS
Reiji Kawaguchi: 'Tony Cragg: Photosynthesis by Consciousness'. *Tony Cragg*. Kanransha Gallery, Tokyo.
Tony Cragg: exhibition catalogue. Kölner Kunstverein.
Pat Turner: 'Tony Cragg's Axehead'. *Tate New Art/The Artist's View*.

1985
ARTICLES
Waldemar Januszczak: 'The Church of the New Art. *Flash Art*. January.
Luciana Rogozinski: 'Tony Cragg – Galleria Tucci Russo'. *Artforum*. March.
Mary Rose Beaumont: review of Lisson Gallery exhibition. *Arts Review*. 12 April.
Monica Petzel: review. *Art Monthly*. May.
Charles Harrison and Judy Annear: view of Hayward Annual. *Art Monthly*. June.
Judith Russi Kirshner: 'Tony Cragg – Richard Deacon'. *Artforum*. Summer.
Isabelle Lemaître: 'Tony Cragg – You don't what you are looking at'. *Artefactum*. November.

ESSAYS
Michael Newman: *The British Show*. Art Gallery of New South Wales and The British Council, London.
Annelie Pohlen: 'Possibilities and new ways: Tony Cragg's sculptures as experience made real' (interview with Demosthenes Davvetas). *Tony Cragg*. Palais des Beaux-Arts, Brussels; ARC, Paris.
Tony Cragg: exhibition catalogue. Tucci Russo Gallery, Torino.

1986
ARTICLES
Care Haenlein: 'Tony Cragg – Protokoll eines Ausstellungsausbaus'. *Nike Wiss Magazine*, Munich.

ESSAYS
Tony Cragg, Demosthenes Davvetas, Carl Haenlein: *Tony Cragg Skulpturen*. Kestner Gesellschaft, Hannover.
Sonsbeek '86. International Sculpture Exhibition. Arnhem, Holland.

1987
ARTICLES
Mary Rose Beaumont: 'Beyond Tradition: Sculpture since Caro'. *20th Century British Art and Design*. February.
Didier Semin: review of the Hayward Gallery exhibition. *Art Press*. July-August.
Paul Bonaventura: *Artefactum*. September-October.

ESSAYS
'Tony Cragg'. *British Art of the 1980s*. Liljevalchs Konsthall. Stockholm.
'Tony Cragg Interviewed by Lynne Cooke' and Lynne Cooke 'Tony Cragg: Thinking Models'. Hayward Gallery exhibition catalogue. Arts Council of Great Britain.

1988
ARTICLES
Eleanor Heartney: 'Born Again Objects'. *Art in America*. February.
Tony Cragg: 'Tony Cragg'. *Artforum*. March.